THE RHYTHM OF GOD

Other Books by GEDDES MACGREGOR

THE RHYTHM OF GOD

A PHILOSOPHY OF WORSHIP

Geddes MacGregor

A CROSSROAD BOOK

The Seabury Press · New York

The Seabury Press
815 Second Avenue
New York, N.Y. 10017

Copyright © 1974 by The Seabury Press, Inc.
Designed by Paula Wiener
Printed in the United States of America

Library of Congress Cataloging in Publication Data

MacGregor, Geddes.
    The rhythm of God.

    "A Crossroad book."
    1. Public worship. I. Title.
BV15.M28   264   74-13598
ISBN 0-8164-1174-3

TO MY BROTHER PRIESTS EVERYWHERE

UT VERITATEM DILIGANT

CONTENTS

Chapter I

THE OLD AND THE NEW

Young folks are smart, but all ain't good thet's
new, I guess the gran'thers they knowed sun-
thin' tu.
—James Russell Lowell, *The Bigelow Papers*

WE happen to live at a time of extreme polarization of
old and new. That does not mean our age is radically different from all others. It does mean that, for historically
understandable reasons, an element common to all ages is
conspicuously characteristic of ours.

Our plight is compounded by the sad circumstance that
large numbers of people try to live outside the historical
dimension and then complain they find life flat. They
want to live in the present; but nobody can live in the
present any more than anyone can live in the future or the
past. To try to live exclusively in the present is as unreal-
istic an aim as is the no less romantic one of trying to live
exclusively in the past. The reason is simple. The present
can no more be captured and lived in than a cinemato-
graphic picture can stand still yet move. You can take a still
picture out of it; but the still is dead. To try to live only in

the present is to die as surely as if we were trying to live
in the past. We can live only in the flow of time, which is
always moving from the past to the future. The present,
the "now," is an artificial abstraction of the mind marking
an imaginary division between past and future, as if the
"now" could be separated from them as the period of time
we call "today" can be separated from yesterday and tomorrow. There is no "now." There is only the dynamic
movement of history. Unless we grasp that fact, we shall
never understand the bases of corporate worship.

I begin, therefore, with some introductory reflections
on the old and the new. For before we attempt to conduct
our inquiry, we should see how the vitality of Christian
liturgy is appropriated through living in that historical dimension in which old and new are recognized to be mere
abstractions, incapable of being concretely separated.

First we may consider the role of liturgy in the life of
the Church in New Testament times. When St. Paul went
on his missionary journeys throughout the Mediterranean
lands, preaching to the church at Corinth and Ephesus
and Rome, there was one item of baggage he did not
carry that any modern missionary would account standard equipment: the New Testament. St. Paul had no copy
of it, of course, for it was not yet written. He was in process of helping to write it. His letters, eagerly awaited and
lovingly read in the various churches he visited, constitute
part of it.

This fact serves to remind us that the Christian Church
is older than the Bible as we know it today. The Bible
readings that are used liturgically at the Eucharist today,
traditionally called the Epistle and the Gospel, are prod-
ucts of the Christian Church. Yet when we go to church
and hear a reading from one of the Epistles and one of the

Gospels, we are brought very close to what Christian worship was like when many Christian communities had to worship in secret. The earliest Christians, however, were Jews, and Christian worship was at first based in part on the sacramental happening in the Upper Room, the night before our Lord's crucifixion, and in part on the synagogue service of the day. People did not sit down to work out a liturgy any more than they sat down to work out a creed. Liturgies and creeds spring up in a "wild" state at first, as do roses and lilies. The eglantine, or wild rose, that grows as a wayside hedge in England is very lovely and gives great charm to rolling English lanes; but because there is a wild rose is no reason not to cultivate the magnificent rose gardens that have been developed. The cultivated rose has a very different kind of beauty.

Christian liturgy is the expression of love, the love of Christ. The word "liturgy," from the Greek, means literally "the people's work": liturgy is the labor of love that all the people do. The priest is at the center of it; but it is everybody's work of love. It is naturally conservative. Even ordinary human love, as it deepens, evokes very conservative sentiments. If you have been married for twenty-two years and have celebrated every previous wedding anniversary with red roses, you are not likely to want to change to white camellias on your twenty-second. In every well-knit family, tradition dies hard. People naturally tend to conserve what they love. A family likes things done as they were done by grandfather and great-grandfather, including even the mistakes. That helps to conserve family sentiment, which is very precious to those who love the family. It is a work of love. It is essential for the Church. It keeps love going. Yet it does not make it grow. Love needs also to be constantly enriched by new life. Love's old story must be told in new ways, and the pledges of love must be renewed daily. So with the Church. We need both old liturgy and new life.

What begins as a purely utilitarian practice or even a mere accident is sometimes continued as a ritual of love. In my student days I was an active member of a society founded in 1764, during Edinburgh's golden age as a literary center. Though the society's library and lobby are electrically lighted, the main hall, where the meetings are held, has never departed from candlelight. The president's desk, and the lectern from which papers are read, are each equipped with a pair of candles, and overhead is the traditional candelabrum.

A history of the society published in 1905 records as follows the failure of a brash and abortive attempt to introduce gas lighting into the precincts of the society.

In 1837 gas was introduced into the Society's rooms. It was lighted in the Hall on the evening of November 28. After a keen debate, the new-fangled illuminant was pronounced a failure and banished to the library and lobby, and the old gilded chandelier was restored to its place. The historic chandelier is the oldest of the Society's possessions; it is our very Palladium; and it is to be hoped it is now safe for all time coming. It holds sixteen candles. By an ancient custom of the Society one of these candles is left unlighted on Tuesday evenings. This custom has been the subject of learned investigation and of the report of a committee.[1]

The latest edition of the society's *History* offers what it accounts the least implausible of various traditional

---

[1] *The History of the Speculative Society, 1764–1904* (Edinburgh: T. and A. Constable, 1905), pp. 25 f.

theories on the subject: "During the Napoleonic Wars Mr. Pitt appealed to the country to save fuel and light. This appeal was conjoined with the new-found and exorbitant imposition on personal income in the slogan 'Less wax, more tax.'" The number of candles was reduced from sixteen to fifteen, and on the termination of the war with Napoleon "that same absence of mind, which in governmental circles omitted to repeal the wartime income tax" caused the society to continue by force of habit the practice of leaving one of the sixteen candle-sockets unfilled.[2]

I have used this example to illustrate that love is the basic factor in making people conservative. Yet love's conservatism is the product of growth. The use of candles on Christian altars originated in the need for light. Much as we have continued the use of candles for dinner, at any rate on festive occasions, so have we continued their use in the Christian liturgy. People gradually came to read into this traditional usage, however, various new meanings, some of them highly novel and complex, as for instance a medieval interpretation, which not only presented the light of the candle as the life of Christ shining in the world but associated the wax of the candle with the Virgin Mary by an elaborate symbolism connected with the virgin bee! The beautiful traditional practice of carrying lighted tapers to the place of the reading of the Gospel symbolizes for us, as it has symbolized for others in ages long past, the new dimension created by the light that has been shed in the world as the Gospel was carried, first from Jerusalem northward and then to the ends of the earth.

In the Middle Ages an extraordinarily complicated net-

---

2 *History of the Speculative Society: Bicentenary Edition* (Edinburgh: T. and A. Constable, 1968), pp. 128 f.

work of symbolic imagery was evolved, including, for instance, whole gardens in honor of the Virgin Mother, arranged in such a way as to exhibit innumerable aspects of medieval devotion to her. There is even a modern American society that will show you how to plant a Lady Garden in your own back yard. It may seem to some an affectation today, like a collection of various kinds of old lavender or the resurrection of the Victorian lover's language of flowers. It shows, nevertheless, the persistence of antique symbolism in the human mind. Come what may, people will always go on using one sort of symbolism or another, and they will always have taste, good or bad. The question is only whether you want your symbolism rich and your taste discriminating or prefer to have a crude taste and a symbolism that is lifeless because suffering from malnutrition. Though I see some fine things in churches done today in modern art-forms, I must admit that others do look to me undernourished in the wisdom of our Christian heritage.

If you examine the liturgical reforms effected at any point in the history of the Church, you will find that their achievement took a long time, sometimes several centuries. You will also find that the language, though it was intended to help bring the liturgy up to date, was probably just a little old-fashioned at the start. The story of the making of the King James Version of the English Bible exemplifies the principle. The translators were under strict rules. They were required (*a*) to use the best scholarship of the day to correct the existing version of the English Bible wherever accuracy demanded a change and also (*b*) to refrain from changing anything that did not strictly require change. The result was, on the one hand, an English that was already slightly antique when the

King James Version appeared in 1611 and, on the other, a version that has been more influential on our modern English language than anything else in our literature, even Shakespeare. The King James Version, though now out of date in terms of biblical scholarship, remains a monument of literary genius, beauty, and power.

The Book of Common Prayer, like the English Bible, is a member of a family with a common ancestry. Its beautiful language echoes its predecessors'. Cranmer's seventeenth-century cadences have incalculably helped, like the Bible itself, to preserve in modern English the robust grandeur that has made the further development of our language possible without degeneration and decay. Behind it lie a thousand years and more of Latin, for this book, valued by all the educated English-speaking world and prized by Anglicans more than anything else in their heritage except the Bible itself, had a long history before it was rendered into English. The terseness of the collects is due not only to an English verbal grace: it is an inheritance from the celebrated linguistic economy of the Latin mold out of which these ancient prayers of the church were cast. At the same time, other parts of our liturgical heritage, such as the so-called Nicene Creed, still reflect something of the different, Attic quality of Greek, more elegant and flowing. Finally, the vigorous earthiness of the Bible and the Prayer Book alike springs from the church's Hebrew heritage, reminding us of the day-to-day, down-to-earth realism of that remarkable people who learned to know God through strife and hardship on the edge of the death-dealing desert. Truly the whole English-speaking world can say, in the language of the Book of Common Prayer: "The lot has fallen unto me in a fair ground; yea, I have a goodly heritage" (Psalm 16:7).

Along with this liturgical possession we inherit also certain traditional patterns of church life, which are not entirely separable from what I have just been discussing, for liturgy and life go hand in hand. When we look at liturgy and life together, however, we find we are prone to imagine that certain traditional practices are more ancient than in fact they are, or that there is some fundamental reason against changing them even when common sense demands change. One of the most remarkable twists in the psychology of tradition is that the newer the tradition the more steadfastly people resist changing it. In ancient universities such as Oxford and Cambridge the recently founded colleges are often more tenacious of their traditions than are the older foundations, some of which date back to the thirteenth century, with roots that are earlier still. Understandably so: they feel less completely secure than do their older sisters. The older colleges are even trying to get away from tradition, in some cases, and cannot always contrive to do so. In the Church, too, people cling desperately to traditions that may be less than fifty years old, as though the whole Church would totter and expire if anyone ever deviated from a practice that began within the lifetime of some of our contemporaries. Consider only how some people cling to Gothic as if God could not be properly worshiped in any other kind of building, though Gothic is a relatively late arrival on the Christian scene and a very regional one at that. Whatever its origin, it is more suited to the somber skies of Germany and England and Maine than to the open sunshine of California and Italy and Greece. Even the use of the wafer of unleavened bread at Holy Communion is no more than a thousand years old at the most, and while that is enough to make a Catholic think many times before seeking to change it, it should not be enough to make the occasional use of the common loaf unthinkable.

What of the parish itself? It is indeed a very ancient unit in the institutional organization of the Christian Church, and it has served well for centuries. Is it really, however, to be accounted quite immutable? In agricultural communities it was a natural and efficient territorial division of the work of the Church. The parish church was the center of all life. The shadow of its dome or spire fell upon the marketplace, and you couldn't buy or sell an egg without the Cross, emblem of our salvation, standing high above you, while the figures of the saints of old looked down on everything you did. Malefactors sought sanctuary in the parish church, for the church was the home of both saint and sinner. It was the focus of all life in all life's multifariousness. The Industrial Revolution, which Trevelyan called "the most important movement in English social history since the Saxon conquest," [3] brought the beginning of a change that took a long time to become noticeable. With the rise of many large cities in the nineteenth century, however, the function of the parish in urban areas could not possibly remain the same, and in an extremely pluralistic society like America it has rarely been anything at all like what it was designed for. The modern city parish is more of a station where people from a wide area focus a certain amount of their attention. Every priest and pastor of such a parish knows that the congregation committed to his charge and the work they do bears little relation to the territorial unit for which he is responsible. In a pluralistic society the relation could not possibly be more than nominal. So the life

[3] G. M. Trevelyan, *English Social History* (London: Longmans, Green and Co., 3rd ed., 1946), p. 371.

of the congregation is inevitably an artificial creation. Even when the congregation is lively and deeply Christian it cannot avoid becoming something of a holy club, and in less fortunate cases it can even become a club that is less than holy. When a congregation becomes a club it always becomes a second-rate club, holy or otherwise. Why? Because the Church is by her nature a missionary body, and it is unnatural for her to be anything else. Her function is not only to feed the sheep but to bring others to the Fold.

How is new life brought into the Church? Not by throwing tradition out the window. Dean Inge once reminded a university congregation that Christ's enemies were "the formally strict traditionalists, the Pharisees." [4] These traditionalists who were so hostile to Christ were legalists. Legalists love tradition for the wrong reasons. They use it as the protector of their vested interests. Good men love tradition only as it is midwife to new birth.

New life is brought into the Church when men and women use ancient traditions well. A green spring shoot does not grow out of midair: it grows out of a healthy old tree, and it never looks fresher than when it grows out of an old tree that has been tended and loved for generations. Trees do need pruning; but we have to prune them carefully from the bottom up, not from the top down. The Church has been pruning our liturgical tree for a long time, and though there are wild branches, it is not really difficult to see the general shape of the main trunk. That is where we must look for the life of the tree. Yet of course nobody is really much interested in the tree trunk

[4] W. R. Inge, *Things New and Old,* as quoted in Horton Davies, *Varieties of English Preaching,* 1900-1960 (Englewood Cliffs, N.J.: Prentice-Hall, 1963), p. 86.

itself. What we want to find in a tree is the foliage, the new life. Some of the new shoots may take odd shapes; but so long as the tree is pruned in the proper places, the new growth will adjust all right in time. New growth on a tree that has been loved and cared for is gracious as well as spontaneous. The pattern of the new growth needs a watchful eye, however, lest it issue in an ungainly shape.

The history of the Church in the United States differs sharply from its history in Europe. In Europe the Church, in her various branches, grew out of an engrafting onto pre-Christian, pagan culture. In southern Europe, on the site of an ancient Roman temple was sometimes built a Christian church of the same general design. In northern Europe, a great church might be built on the site of an old Druid temple. The old gods were christianized, sometimes rather superficially, as in the case of Santa Claus, but always in such a way as to exhibit the continuity of the pagan past with the Christian present. The far north was christianized very late. Christianity did not reach Scandinavia till a thousand years after the time of Christ, and in Sweden its advent was especially belated. In the Scandinavian sagas we read of how one of the old gods would appear to mariners, lamenting the fact that he was growing old. He was being retired. There was no longer any place left for him. So saying he would jump overboard, never to be seen again, leaving behind him only a wistful memory. That wistfulness for the pagan past has always haunted Europe and has given even her secularism a special character. In Europe the very notion of "going secular" carries with it at least a distant echo of the pagan past and often entails a real sense of reversion to that earlier historical root.

In America, on the contrary, Christianity in all its

forms came already packaged. It was not engrafted upon
a native culture. It was an import. This circumstance has
had an enormous effect upon the development of church
life here. On the one hand, America has always tended to
invest its nationalistic culture with a sort of religious aura,
half tribal, half Christian. This characteristic generally
dismays Europeans, who usually misunderstand it. What
seems to them America's almost infinite capacity for flag-
waving at every conceivable opportunity suggests to Europeans merely a lack of national self-confidence. Then,
on the other hand, America has tended to secularize
Christianity; that is, to adapt it to American culture. This,
too, Europeans generally misunderstand, taking it to be
merely a cheap, not to say blasphemous, watering down
of Christianity. Another way of putting all this is to say
that America has a semicultural religion in a semireligious
culture. In Europe there has generally been a greater tension between religion and culture because Christianity
has tended to be seen as making inroads, slowly and not
always successfully, into nationalistic cultures over the
course of many centuries. In America, though there have
been the tensions inevitable in any highly pluralistic society, there has not been the same tension between religion
and culture, just because people brought their particular
forms of Christianity to the country of their adoption as
they brought their other luggage, and then set about
americanizing what they had brought, as they american-
ized their speech and their dress.

In many ways the effect of this Americanization of
Christianity has been good. For example, it has eventually
softened some of the asperities of theological controversy
and in recent years it has greatly assisted popular participation in ecumenical conversations. At its best it has en-

riched Christianity, as Socratic humanism enriched it in Europe. In other ways, however, the effect has been less happy. For there has been a strong danger of subordinating Christianity to nationalism, which is the way to political absolutism and totalitarianism. Since there is less awareness of the ancient roots of our Christian heritage, there is a very real danger of simply dissolving Christianity in a nationalistic saucepan, till there is little left of the Christian heritage but a vague flavor running through the national culture. When this begins to happen, people feel the ancient heritage of Christian doctrine and liturgy remote not only from daily life but also from that vapid watered-down Christianity that is frequently offered as the essence of faith, though it is in fact merely a lingering aroma of one of its impoverished manifestations.

We hear a great deal in certain quarters about getting down to grass roots; but grass roots are at far too superficial a level for what is needed. We are not dealing with grass but with a tree whose roots are not only ancient but widespread and deep. Educated people can usually make sense of the antiquity; they cannot always so easily grasp the continuity and depth. Then again, Christianity is nothing if not international. As soon as it is perverted to something national, it is a parody of itself, even at the best. It is also continuous. The Anglican tradition, for example, provides a *model* of the notion of continuity: the notion of apostolic succession through bishops. Yet this notion, when mechanistically interpreted, falls far short of presenting an adequate idea of the mysterious reality of continuous life.

Only in the measure in which ordinary people have a deep sense of that oneness with a great and beloved

Christian family that has spanned the centuries can their liturgy be an effective expression of Christian faith and love. Liturgical leaders, if they are to succeed in their task, must enable the average worshiper to become acutely aware that he belongs to a family that has joyed and sorrowed both in the Roman Catacombs and in the palaces of the Tudor kings, both in the sumptuous cathedrals and abbeys of the High Middle Ages and on the hillsides and glens where the Scottish Covenanters foregathered, a family that has spread to every corner of the earth.

In Europe, in the eighteenth century, Christianity seemed doomed to speedy and total extinction. Then, in the nineteenth century, miracles happened. The Roman Church, which had become a shadow of her former self, was spectacularly revived. Protestantism expanded, as never before in history, to the ends of the earth. The Anglican Communion, seemingly dying of spiritual torpor, was not only restored through the miracle of the Oxford Movement, but acquired a new *kind* of vitality beyond anything the typical nineteenth-century Tractarian could have easily imagined. In every case you will find, despite the great differences in style, that each branch of the Church achieved its renaissance through bringing about a deepened sense of belonging to a great heritage. To commemorate the early saints of the Church at Rome, such as Clement and Cyprian, along with Aunt Bessie and Uncle Bob, and to see the vast procession of God's warriors marching ahead of one's own private heroes of the faith, is the first step toward making liturgy come to life.

The sense of the splendor of our Christian heritage and of its universality and power is not merely something to be cultivated from time to time. It ought to shine through *all* worship. Of course there are some points in our liturgy at which it emerges with specially dazzling beauty and compelling force. The genius of Wesley has captured something of that beauty in his incomparable hymns. The Scottish Kirk once captured something of it in the slow tempo and solemn rhythm of the metrical psalter. The liturgy of the French Reformed Church captures something of it in the majestic recognition of the abasement of all creatures in the presence of the Sovereign Lord of all. Can any Christian be so insensitive as not to feel the thrill of participating in a great work when the priest invites the faithful to join themselves not only with the whole Church of all climes and all ages but with the very angels of heaven? All the Church's poetry is here, and the impact of it is almost unbearably beautiful. A priest was asked: "How many people were at the early celebration of the Eucharist last Wednesday morning?" He replied: "There were three old ladies, the janitor, several thousand archangels, a large number of seraphim, and several million of the triumphant saints of God." All this comes home to us vividly when the priest, having declared that it is very meet, right, and our bounden duty to give thanks to God, joins to him not only us but (as the ancient lovely phrase has it) "all the company of heaven." This sense of belonging to a far greater community than meets the eye ought to pervade our worship at every point. Throughout the entire eucharistic service we are, in the biblical phrase, "encompassed about by a great cloud of witnesses."

No one who has really taken possession of his Christian heritage need ever feel the need to go to a spiritistic séance to meet his loved ones who have relinquished this life and gone into the fuller life beyond. They are accessible to him at every eucharistic service. There, at the family meal of the whole Church, he can find his loved ones. Where else should he find them but at the place that they and he most deeply love, the altar of God, whereon is spread the holy eucharistic feast? Where do we go to find a friend we want to encounter? Surely at the place most important for him to be, the place he loves best. At the altar of God, then, not in the house of strangers, should a Christian find those whose presence he seeks. There, if anywhere at all, he can indeed encounter them. There only will his aching heart know rest and peace.

How shall we keep the Church's liturgy and life from turning into an empty, meaningless routine? The answer is simple: by investing it daily with the new life that springs from the presence of the Holy Spirit in our hearts, that presence which Christ himself has promised us. An ancient ritual, if ever it was expressive of eternal truth, need never pall, unless we let it. The golden letters of God's Word need never tarnish, if only we keep them burnished in our hearts, so illuminating our lives, which may well be the only Bible our neighbor will ever know. A great story, if it contains truth, need never grow stale. Do we stop going to see *Hamlet* because it must be out of date by now? No; we find better and better performers. Do we take down the "Mona Lisa" from the Louvre and throw it in the trash because it is old-fashioned? Of course not: we find new ways of looking at and interpreting the same old picture. In Christian worship we should keep the traditional *shape;* but we can and must infuse into it the new life that the Holy Spirit of God is ever making available to his Church and that manifests itself in many new patterns.

We are all very anxious, and rightly so, to prevent our congregations from becoming old people's homes. The

Church must not neglect the elderly, not least because without the wisdom of the elderly we shall be very poor indeed. Yet to draw young people toward the Church, both those of definitely Christian background and the far more numerous segment of today's youth that lacks that advantage, is a totally indispensable part of the Church's mission to the world. We hear on all sides that the archaic cast of thought and picturesque but outmoded language of the Bible and the Prayer Book are all but meaningless to the young people of today. True, they were almost as archaic to the average Victorian child as they are to the average young person today; but the Victorian child was for various reasons encouraged to understand their beauty, while the inescapable fact is that the young person of today is not. So the Church tries, sometimes a little frantically, not to say pathetically, to appeal to him.

Suppose, however, that you examine, say, the liturgical revisions experimentally proposed by the General Convention of the Episcopal Church in America in 1968. These proposed revisions were generally understood to be instruments for catching the younger and more "worldly" people who were thought to be somehow or other too small or too agile for Cranmer's net. Nevertheless, you will find that the most admirable and effective revisions therein offered are in fact much more old-fashioned than Cranmer. For instance, the magnificent litaneutical Prayer of Intercession beginning, "In peace, let us pray to the Lord," is a thousand years older than the Book of Common Prayer and considerably older than the Roman Missal.

The Roman Church, as part of her own campaign for streamlining her liturgy, is using a shorter form of words in administering the sacrament: "The Body of Christ" with the response, "Amen." Some may take this to be an ultra-modern simplification, a drastic excision of antique flummery to meet the tastes of modern youth. In fact, however, it is far older than the more discursive traditional Anglican and Roman forms. It is mentioned by St. Augustine nearly sixteen hundred years ago as the normal form in his day. In a sermon he tells the people: "When the priest gives you the Sacrament, saying, 'The Body of Christ,' and you say, 'Amen,' *be* the Body of Christ, so that your 'Amen' may be true." Here, then, is a typical modern liturgical revision, up to date and "with it," which in fact is a thousand years older than the form it is replacing. Again, while the Roman Church has turned most of the Latin Mass into the vernacular, Anglicans, in their liturgical experiments, offer the people a little Greek: instead of "Lord, have mercy upon us," they can now have "Kyrie eleison." You may regard this as more "groovy" than Cranmer; but of course it was already old hat in the Christian Church before the English language was born, and even, indeed, before some Christians started using Latin.

The truth is, of course, that the very ancient may be far more "with it" and much more "swinging" than the language of last year. A teenager may find himself better attuned to his great-grandparents than to the parents against whom he is rebelling. A boy who would not be caught dead with his father's style of haircut sallies forth happily wearing his great-grandfather's, which his grandfather would not have been caught dead in. Antiquity has very little to do with "square" or "groovy." What matters is merely whether you are indentified with the enemy or not, and the enemy, of course, is the generation against whom you are rebelling. Few children have anything in particular against anybody older than their parents.

With all this in mind, we may well note that when new

life is infused into the Church by the needs of young people and, one hopes, their abundant presence, there exists
an admirable opportunity to restore to the Church some
of her forgotten treasures that for long have been known
only to scholars. In the ordinary life of the parish, these
treasures have been virtually lost. Nothing would be more
foolish than to strip the Church of her heritage under pretext of accommodating her life to that of the rising generation. That would be the way to alienating young people
and the world at large far more surely and permanently
than they are now alienated. Within the treasures of our
own heritage, however, we can find much that, being un-
tainted by association with the recent past, can be used to
captivate the hearts of the many young people in our time
who are longing for a way in which they may be a part of
the life of the Church without its entailing a tie with their
parents, which is in many cases, at any rate, the only aspect of Christianity that they account really unendurable.

If we truly believe in the presence of the Risen Christ,
the question can never be: "How can we accommodate
Christianity to the tastes of a new generation that seems
disinclined for it?" To put that question is indeed the surest way to incur the contempt of all honest people, young
and old. For to ask such a question is to demonstrate
clearly that you really don't believe a word you say about
the Gospel and the Church. No, the question must be,
rather: "How can we make the ancient glories of the
Church shine anew in our own age?"

The simple answer is both the most profound and the
most effective: we can make the ancient glories shine in
our time by being as scrupulously honest in our appreciation of them as was our Lord himself in his appreciation
of the values of his Hebrew heritage. Our Lord studied
his heritage as all men study what they truly love. He in-

culcated a great respect for it: "Do not suppose," he said,
"that I have come to abolish the Law and the prophets; I
did not come to abolish, but to complete" (Matthew 5:17,
NEB). But he also taught that we are not to attend to the
outside of the cup and let the inside go dirty. "Blind Phar-
isee! Clean the inside of the cup first; then the outside
will be clean also" (Matthew 23:25, NEB). We must get
right to the heart of our heritage and see that what we are
preserving is really the essential. And how shall we know
if not by diligent and earnest prayer that we may be given
a taste for the Church's poetry? For it is only through such
a gift that we shall learn what is living and what is dead
in the tree that is the Church.

Once we seize hold of the life of the Church, which is
none other than the life of our Risen Lord himself and of
the Holy Spirit that he promised would abide with his
Church till the end of time, the rest will take care of itself.
For then we shall be no more in danger of mistaking what
is mere dross for what is the very stuff of our faith than
we are in danger of mistaking our collar for our neck.
Could it be that so many young people cannot see the
glories of the Church because we are casting our shadow
upon these glories? If only we show the ancient glories in
our own worship and in our own lives, no one, young or
old, will boggle at the Church's style of dress or speech. "I
shall draw all men to myself," our Lord promised, "when
I am lifted up from the earth" (John 12:32). When we
have lifted Christ up in our lives, the ancient glories of
the Church shall shine brightly enough to bridge any generation gap, and no one will really care if the language we
use be as archaic as Chaucer's or our clothes as old-
fashioned as Abraham's.

Chapter II

LITURGY AND THE
PARTICULARITY PRINCIPLE

"The individual"—with this category the cause
of Christianity stands or falls. . . . Without
this category pantheism has triumphed abso-
lutely.

—Søren Kierkegaard, *The Point of View*

THE fundamental characteristic of all worship is adoring
love. Worship has this characteristic whether it is Hindu
or Muslim, Jewish or Christian. The Mahayana worshiper
who seeks to identify himself with the eternal Buddha-
nature, no less than the Jewish one who bends in awe before the eternal Thou, engages in an act of homage, directed at what he takes to be Supreme Being. If he be so
inclined he may give his concept of that Being some metaphysical articulation. He may specify the focus of his
worship as the Absolute, the Eternal, the Creator, the
Trinity, the Sovereign King of the Universe. If, again, he
is of an emotional disposition, he is likely to pour forth
loving superlatives in abundant profusion. Whatever his
philosophical acumen, whatever his personal tempera-
ment, his worship will always be essentially adoration.

It will be essentially an act of adoration whether it is

personal prayer in the secrecy of his own room or corporate prayer in temple, synagogue, or church. For various
reasons, however, the element of adoration may be sometimes partially obscured in private prayer by a large number of other legitimate but not essential elements. In such
prayer the worshiper will open his heart to God, possibly
in very colloquial ways. He will intercede for his needy
friends, ask for personal graces, beg for special favors.
There is a place in liturgical worship, too, for such inter-
cessory and petitionary prayer; but while private prayer
need not always make the essential element of adoration
explicit, liturgical worship that fails to make it central
becomes a mere caricature of itself. When church worship
becomes predominantly a place of preaching or edification or moralizing or socializing or the cult of mere
beauty, it ceases to fulfill the one function that makes it
indispensable to Christian life. When corporate worship is
bereft of explicit adoration, it soon degenerates into twaddle, and other people's twaddle usually sounds less tolera-
ble than one's own. The Church must indeed proclaim the
gospel and do so with mighty power. The Church must
certainly teach and edify, and the Christian community
must by all means show, as no other community has the
capacity to show so well, "how good, how delightful it is
for all to live together like brothers" (Psalm 133:1, Jerusalem Bible). The House of God, even at its most austere,
has a beauty no other building can possess. Yet when all
that is said, the Church is never so much herself and never
commands with such authenticity as when she shouts:
Venite adoremus! Come, let us adore!

Venite adoremus. The verb *adorare*, to adore, is transi-
tive. Grammatically, in English as in Latin, it requires an
object, and the grammatical convention is well grounded.

What, then, do Christians adore when they respond to the call to worship? In common with all worshipers of every sort, they worship that which they take to be the core of reality, the deepest reality they are able to recognize. The individual's response is the measure of his ability to take a theocentric view of life. Of course, like the rest of us, he is impeded by his own self-centeredness in all its manifestations. He may not be able to see far beyond the pool in which, like Narcissus, he is constrained to look and into which he often gazes with pathetic intensity, finding nothing but his own little self, or at most what the psychoanalysts tell him, with accurate enough reporting, in his superego. Even the saintliest and most adventuresome Christian cannot hope entirely to escape the natural human tendency to stay within the prison of his own self. Nevertheless, the target of liturgical worship is always the ontological reality which, recognized as the Other, stoops over and over again in humble accommodation to our myopia.

The worshiper, in acknowledging the ontological reality he adores, recognizes that it is coming to meet him before he is going to meet it. In the language of piety, God speaks and acts before I do. Theologians call God's action "prevenient," meaning that it precedes in every way the response it makes possible. Some Christians have felt the sense of that prevenience so vividly that they have accounted the proper attitude toward God to be nothing other than a silent waiting. Such an attitude, which historians of Christian mystical piety call Quietism, fails fully to appreciate the nature of adoring love. Genuine love does not wait frigidly for the lover to woo but goes forth in loving response, confidently knowing that the lover is already on his way. So the worshiper, in crying, "Holy,

Holy, Holy, Lord God of Sabaoth," knows that he does
not intrude upon the privacy of God, for in daring to utter
these words in love he confidently recognizes that God
has already given himself to be adored. That God so
makes himself available is the primary cause of the worshiper's rejoicing.

Yet the response of the worshiper to the divine prevenience is no more restricted to formal adoration than the
response of the beloved is restricted to a formal
acknowledgment and acceptance of the lover. The worshiper pours forth his whole being, uttering his hopes and
fears, begging forgiveness for his follies, acknowledging
his personal unworthiness, asking favors for his friends,
remembering also the friends he has loved and lost
through death, opening his heart in every way to the
Eternal, the One in whom alone he can put his total trust.
He sums up his love in one attitude, which is the hallmark
of authentic love: sacrifice. His response is a response in
which he offers all that he has.

Primitive people, in token of the sacrifice that is essential to the loving response of all genuine worship, offered
prized possessions: their best sheep, the first fruits of the
harvest, even (as Abraham was willing to do) an only son.
In later biblical times, sacrifices of that kind, which are a
common feature of the great religions of the world at one
time or another, came to be denounced, not because worship does not entail sacrifice, but because such sacrifice is
not enough for God. It also makes him who offers it
highly susceptible to cheating and self-deception, for he is
prone to sacrifice what he does not really need, so that it
is no sacrifice at all but only a make-believe. The one who
makes it is somewhat like the man whom Deutero-Isaiah
so eloquently pillories, who hews down a tree; takes most

of it to make a fire, partly to warm himself and partly to
bake bread; and then, using what is left over, makes an
idol before which he falls down, demanding deliverance
of the god he has fashioned by his skill in carpentry (Isa-
iah 44:13–17). So the later Hebrew writers protest as does
the Psalmist, that God is not pleased with "burnt
offerings" and that

The sacrifice acceptable to God is a broken spirit;
    a broken and contrite heart, O God, thou wilt not despise.
                                            Psalm 51:17, RSV

Christian worship has always recognized, of course,
that principle, so well ingrained into the Hebrew tradition
whence Jesus came. Nevertheless, Christian focus on the
presence of the Risen Christ in the midst of the Church
has brought about a very sophisticated interpretation of
the nature and place of sacrifice in liturgical worship. Not
only is the old sacrifice of sheep and heifers inadequate;
even a broken and contrite heart is not in itself enough,
however necessary it may be as a preliminary condition.
The loving heart must offer the best there is; and to the
Christian, despite his own spiritual poverty, has been
made available the only offering that could possibly meet
the case: God himself, who gives himself sacramentally in
the Eucharist for the appropriation of the faithful.

Once that principle is fully recognized, no other sacrifice can seem sufficient. We, having nothing of our own,
are like small children dependent on their parents for the
money to buy their parents a present. The parents do not
need or want a present: they need and want the child's
response to their love. God does not need or want anything, so what can his people offer him? The Christian

takes his cue from the revelation that God, in the mysterious outpouring of his love for his creation, has given himself in Christ, so that there is an answer, after all, to the seemingly silly question: What can a theologically sophisticated man or woman dare to offer to God? There is only one gift that would not be an idolatrous sacrifice, namely, God himself, and that is precisely what the sacrament enables us to offer. This gives a special color to the whole of Christian liturgy, as we shall consider later.

For certain understandable reasons, the sixteenth-century Reformers were inclined to abandon the sacrificial aspect of the Mass; but in so doing they deprived Christian liturgical worship of its fundamental character and its characteristic joy. Contrary to what the Reformers tended to fear, the Mass is not at all like either the old temple sacrifices, Jewish or pagan. It is, indeed, the only adequate safeguard against the resuscitation of the idolatry they would now entail. There is no other religion in which provision is made or can be made for such an efficacious safeguard against the foolish idolatries of sacrifice than is provided in the Christian Mass. In terms of sacrificial worship, it is the end not only of the road but of all possible roads. We shall have to consider the significance of this assertion when we discuss the principles of Christian liturgy.

Mohandas Gandhi, the foremost political and religious leader, in modern times, of the religion Westerners call Hinduism, whose writings in the Bhakti tradition brought him the Nobel Prize for literature, used to say that though he did not personally feel the need to worship temple images, he would never wish to deprive others of the right to do so. Christians would do well to note the profundity of Gandhi's remark. It is by no means merely a characteristic expression of the tolerance the textbooks commonly attribute to Hinduism. It calls attention to the fact that, though every embodiment of worship may give rise to idolatry, it does so not because of its concreteness but because of the idolatrous attitude of the worshiper.

A professor may take up a more idolatrous attitude toward his concrete embodiment of worship than does a peasant toward his. Indeed, the "highest" idol, as Kierkegaard and others have much reminded us, may be the worst. More importantly still, we should never forget that all worship has a concrete embodiment of one sort or another, and that concrete embodiment, far from being something to be overcome, is an expression of man's recognition of his creatureliness as an embodied spirit. To try to escape from that condition is the opposite of worship. To accept it with joy is the attitude of humility apart from which worship is impossible.

The spirit of man finds its embodiment in human history, and each individual finds his own embodiment in his personal history. The mystery of the Eternal, who stoops in love to sanctify humanity, comes also to each worshiper as an individual. Corporate worship is therefore not only a joining with our brothers and sisters, the partners in our common human lot as creatures of the one Creator. It is also, and no doubt for most worshipers pre-eminently the individual's expression of his overflowing personal love. Why, then, the liturgy? Why not express his personal love in secret prayer to God in the lonely quiet of his own room in the forest or on the hillside, far from human haunts? Such solitary adoration is indeed worship, and sometimes it can be very great worship; but the genuine lover wants to do more than tell his love in secret places. He wants to tell the world. He wants the whole world to

join with him in celebrating his love. The genuine worshiper, though he deeply cherishes those quiet moments
of private adoration, is happiest when he is able to find a
thousand others with whom to share his joy. For the joy of
worship, even more than the next best spiritual joys of
life, is infinitely multiplied in being shared.

Worship is not easy even for the saintliest of men and
women. For most it is difficult. What more than anything
else makes it difficult is the natural tendency of human
beings to turn in on themselves. Moreover, when we do
overcome our self-centeredness, we do so by opening ourselves to our fellow men, and that has a strong tendency
to make us content to see in others the locus of the
life-giving power that saves us from the agony of our
own in-growing egoism. We may be so appreciative of the
kindness of someone who does us a small favor in time of
need that we forget the larger scene, the divine activity
that made that kindness possible.

A few are so soured in life as to see everthing grossly
distorted, perhaps leaving their whole fortune for the care
of a cat or dog in whom they have found solace, while
leaving their children or close friends in want. Most people see life in a better perspective. Most of us catch
glimpses, at least now and then, of the graciousness of Being, the Being that makes everything else possible, and we
make clumsy attempts to leap beyond our human frame
of reference to that upon which humanity like all else depends for its very existence. Comparatively few of us are
capable of sustained devotion to the Eternal. Liturgical
action provides not only the means of expressing our
devotion, such as it may be; it also furnishes the arena
where we may be trained to focus our eyes on our Creator
and accustom ourselves to sustaining the joy of loving

him. Through liturgy we learn to feel at home with God. For those who long for mystical experience, there is no other avenue that provides such a direct means of training, to prepare them for such experience, than the disciplined love that liturgy demands. Yet mystical experience can never be the chief goal of liturgical worship, the fundamental purpose of which is simply loving and joyous adoration.

There are, indeed, subsidiary aims, such as securing the moral encouragement and support we all need and can obtain through the presence of others who share in doing the same work, the same labor of love. The collects that "collect" the prayers of the people are among the symbols of that important mutual sustenance. I am able to pray in a special way for those who are physically together with me in our common act, and I rejoice to know that I am being upheld by the prayer that others present are also offering for me. Even meeting together may be a good subsidiary purpose. Not only are some people excruciatingly lonely; all of us are in one way or another at least in some measure alienated through self-centeredness and the blind spots that afflict even the most perspicacious among us. To join with others in hearing the gospel regularly proclaimed and expounded has great value to those who are trying to tread the difficult path of faith.

Yet the moment that any one of these subordinate ends obscures in even the slightest degree the central purpose of corporate worship, the whole concept of churchgoing begins to disintegrate. For these subordinate ends cannot give to churchgoing the *kind* of meaning it needs to sustain it in the world we live in. The meaning they have, though by no means negligible, depends wholly on the value attributed to the central act, which alone confers on

the other subordinate acts whatever value they have. As
soon as the nature of the central purpose of corporate
worship is obscured in any congregation of people, the
life of that congregation is on its way out. It may die with
merciful speed or it may linger on painfully, as so often it
does; but it is in any case on its way to the grave, for it
has lost what it takes to sustain liturgical life.

Apart from such life a parish is no more than a club,
and in such circumstances it is notoriously a third-rate
club at that. It survives only as a hospital might survive
for a time without healing, or a school without education.
Because there are subordinate ends in a college besides education, a college might survive for some time after it had
ceased to fulfill any serious educational purpose. Students
might continue to attend, enjoying the company of their
peers and occasionally of their professors. The professors
would find plenty of things to do in the library and the
lab. The college dining-hall would still serve food. There
would still be pleasant chatter in the dorms. The college
bells would still tintinnabulate. No doubt there would still
be commencement addresses and perhaps elegantly inscribed parchments; but one day someone would at last
ask the question: "Why are we here?" No one could satis-
factorily answer him; but that would not matter. He
would have accomplished his mission. For merely by asking the question he would perturb others who in turn
would ask it too, till at length everybody would be asking
it. By that time the fun of meeting for lunch would have
faded, the attraction of the library would have diminished, and the pleasure of chattering in the dorms would
have palled. At last the enrollment would be so atten-
uated that the college would not be able to pay even its
light bill.

That is, of course, in essence the tragic history of a thousand parishes. They forgot the one purpose on which all else depends. The grandest eloquence, the warmest togetherness, and the prettiest appointments cannot keep a church going. There is no life without liturgy. That is why it is vital not only to have people understand liturgy as the heart of parish life but to assert its supremacy with passionate, evangelical zeal, in season and out of season. Few people understand the anatomy of congregational life well enough to need anything less than a constant reminder of the function of its heart. We shall discuss the symptoms of liturgical heart disease in a later chapter.

The incitement to liturgical worship always emerges in particularity, in "thisness," in a here-and-now situation. Jacob, as he awoke from his dream, exclaimed: "How awesome is this place. This is none other than the house of God, and this is the gate of heaven" (Genesis 28:17, RSV). The flow of history embodies the Eternal that transcends all history. The oddness of the particularity is inseparable from the embodiment. For Christians the paradigmatic case is the Incarnation: the brief encampment of the Eternal in a specific, even an unlikely isthmus of the sands of time. For some the psychological effect of that particularity is so strong that they find difficulty in recognizing any place other than "this one" as a possible place of encounter with God. George Whitefield, the Calvinist associate of the Wesleys, records that "I know the place; it may be superstitious, but whenever I go to Oxford I cannot help running to the spot where Jesus Christ first revealed himself to me, and gave me the new birth."

The Eastern Church, whose realism in such matters is far too little appreciated in the West, understands well the principle behind such feelings. The Orthodox ikon is

no mere "aid to devotion." St. John Damascene called it a
channel of divine grace. It is to be accounted, by appoint-
ment, a trysting place with God. The ikon is not blessed
at large; it is blessed for a particular church or even for a
particular person, as indeed, in the Latin Church, a rosary
is blessed for the particular individual who is to use it. So
the ikon is not by any means merely a picture to remind
those who may chance upon it to turn their thoughts to
God. *My* ikon is *my* particular vehicle of *my* tryst with
the Eternal. From the patristic period the Platonist presuppositions of Orthodoxy have ensured for the faithful
the sense of movement from the sensuousness of the
image to the spiritual reality that is mirrored in it, while
the oddness and the particularity spring from the Hebrew
and biblical groundwork of the Church's liturgical theology. As our bodies are not nourished by groceries-at-large
but by *this* particular plate of ham and eggs, so our hearts
are not "strangely warmed" by piety in general but in *this*
place, at *this* time, by *this* instrument. Sound, then, is the
instinct that impels the average churchman to think not
only of "his" Bible, "his" Prayer Book, and even (much as
his pastor may deplore it) "his" pew, but also of "his" parish and "his" church, as though he would hardly know
how to worship God anywhere else.

This very parochialism, for all its seemingly absurd narrowness, is an expression of the particularity principle.
The fundamental character of that principle is often obscured by the degraded and perverted forms in which it is
expressed. That is why it often seems natural to reli-
giously minded people to seek for a universality and ecumenicity that is fundamentally alien to the ways of God
with man. Such a quest is based on presuppositions as
radically false as those that misguide so many thoughtful

and scholarly people who, about the turn of the century, hoped to find a common essence that could be distilled out of all religions, a sort of religious Esperanto. Such quests are misguided, not because one way is right and all others wrong but, rather, because they ignore the fundamantal nature of all man's trafficking with God. Yet the quest for universality and timelessness, though its presuppositions are false, is not wholly misguided. The universal and the timeless symbolize the Eternal Thou; but the Eternal Thou cannot be appropriated without the particularization. The disdain we affect for particularity is satanic, because it springs from our unwillingness to acknowledge our creatureliness, and so from our correspondingly strong inclination to wish to identify ourselves with God, which is the worst of all identity mistakes.

Liturgical worship, therefore, though it must symbolize the ontological reality of the Eternal Thou, should so distance the worshiper from it as to make possible his I-Thou encounter. He encounters the Other, the Eternal, in a novel way. Throughout the centuries millions of people have seen daffodils; but no one has seen them as did Wordsworth. Millions have seen larks; but no one as did Shelley. Millions of worshipers have heard the deacon sing the Gospel at Mass; but to no one has it come in exactly the way in which it came to *this* worshiper, speaking to *his* particular, incomparable condition. So while he rejoices that he is one with the millions who have heard that Gospel in precisely these words on the Third Sunday in Lent, he knows there is no other human being who has ever heard it in just this novel, life-giving way, tailor-cut, so to speak, to the clamorous needs of *this* man's situation.

The significance of particularity is a comparatively late discovery of the religious consciousness. The awakening of that consciousness is attended by immense delight in the discovery of the religious dimension, but there is generally an extreme lack of sophistication about harnessing and appropriating religion to human need. The awakening may occur among modern chemists and actuaries and engineers in a society that is technologically advanced as well as among people who are in that respect very primitive. Wherever it occurs, however, people tend to behave as such primitive people behave when they are first confronted with a physical phenomenon such as electricity. After they have overcome their fear of it they want to grab it as a child tries to grab the moon. Not understanding its volatile and other peculiarities, they think they can take it "whole," as we take the air we breathe. They have to learn that it must be stored and channeled so that it comes to us not only in amounts we can take but in a form we can use. It must reach us in a form accommodated to our needs, so that it can light our desk lamp and toast our bread. Otherwise it will kill us.

That is the truth that Moses, like other great religious pioneers, had to learn. When Moses asked Yahweh to show him his glory, Yahweh replied that Moses could not see his face, "for man cannot see me and live" (Exodus 33:18–20). The best Yahweh would do in answer to Moses' entreaty was to let him stand in a crevice of the rock and shield him with his hand while Yahweh passed by. Then Yahweh would take his hand away, and Moses would see Yahweh's back; "but my face is not to be seen" (cf. Exodus 33:21–23). The Eternal One is death to us till, through particularization, he can pass the barbed barricades of the human heart and the narrow, slanted doors of the human mind. That is why Lucretius was right, in a way, in his jibe that religion begins with fear: it does begin with fear, as it develops through particularization, into unspeakable love. As Reinhold Niebuhr robustly expressed this truth: "God must be experienced as 'enemy' before he can be known as friend." [1]

So while liturgy is an act of adoring love, a celebration of our love of God, it is also an actualization of the particularity principle. The Lord is in *this* holy temple. God with *us*. So liturgy, though fundamentally as undidactic as all art, has nevertheless the didactic function that is present in all sacramentalism. In the traditional Catholic pattern of the Mass, this function is especially performed within the pro-anaphora, the Mass of the Catechumens, where the lessons are read, the Gospel proclaimed, and the homily preached. This, too, is part, but only part, of liturgy. It is part of the sacramental mediation of God to us, the accommodation of the Eternal to the little ladles our trembling hands bring to the fearsome Fount of Goodness that God is.

In Catholic tradition no sense is left unassailed by the symbols of the dimension that is opened up to us by the invading God. Yet when the particularization is accomplished in us, thoroughly divesting us of all our foolish pretensions at capturing deity with our tattered net and identifying ourselves with our Creator, the Sovereign King of the Universe, we are not left empty-handed. We can say more than Toplady in his famous hymm:

> Nothing in my hand I bring,
> Simply to thy Cross I cling.

[1] Reinhold Niebuhr, *Faith and History* (New York: Charles Scribner's Sons, 1957), p. 103.

For the Christian can bring that which the Cross of Christ provides: the gift that God has purchased for us to bring, which in the very carrying of it to the altar where the priest offers it in sacrifice, we learn to grow in the costliest of all kinds of love, the love which, even as it hurts most sharply, brings our most perfect healing and our only lasting joy.

Chapter III

LITURGY IS WORK

The real essence of work is concentrated energy.
—Walter Bagehot, *Biographical Studies*

LONG ago, among simple country folk in Presbyterian Scotland, one could still hear the Communion service designated "the Great Work." I remember in my childhood not only hearing an elderly and old-fashioned shepherd so allude to it, but seeing him momentarily and inconspicuously doff his cap as he uttered the words. No more fitting name could easily be found for the central act of Christian worship. It is also a practical one that might be used in reference to what Anglicans today sometimes call the Parish, or Family, Eucharist. That liturgy is work may seem a truism to those who remember that the word means "the work of the people." Yet since that is so often and widely forgotten, a constant reminder is in order.

There is almost nothing, indeed, of which church people need to be so constantly reminded. As other watchwords of the faith, such as "The Lord is King," are openly

inscribed on walls to the glory of God and the edification
of the faithful, so might well be written up for all to see:
"Liturgy is work." It is, of course, a particular kind of
work and should be a specially joyous work. Hard workers
best understand the spirit of liturgy. Those who know
how to work as if they were praying know how to pray as
if prayer were the most joyous work of all. The Benedic-
tines, in prizing their ancient motto, *laborare est orare*, to
work is to pray, recognize well that the public prayer of
the Church is work: it is both the *officium divinum*, the
divine office, and the *opus Dei*, the work of God.

The importance of affirming liturgy as work is likely to
elude us till we see into what absurdities church people
descend as soon as they forget the true character of
churchgoing. When worship is understood as inspirational, the worshipers have to be cajoled into putting
themselves in the way of being inspired. When the performance fails to inspire them they naturally feel cheated,
as one is disappointed in an amusement park that fails to
amuse. Such worship is more catechumenal instruction
than liturgy. While that educational enterprise has its
place in the preparation of every Christian, there is something far wrong when people go through life as regular
churchgoers, yet end as octogenarians whose funeral,
even, is conducted with the same sort of saccharine inani-
ties that have been the stuff of their worship all their
lives. One might conceivably begin to wean a very
nonmilitant atheist from his unbelief with a proposal such
as "Shall we pray?" but to be still doing so fifty years later
is rather like asking a converted cannibal on the golden
jubilee of his baptism, "How about trying a little nonhu-
man flesh today?" If *oremus* is too antique even for a society in which the Hebrew *amen* is understood by the most

unbelieving Gentile, and if "Let us pray" sounds too insipid to those whose grammatical education has not advanced sufficiently to enable them to recognize an imperative, why not a blow from a wooden mallet? It would certainly be better than invitatories such as, "Shall we engage in a little prayer?" which produce the temptation to respond with a resounding "No." Since unruly inclinations tend to beset us all as soon as we begin to engage in the business of worship, I see no point in giving this one a cordial encouragement.

As I have suggested elsewhere,[1] instead of cajoling devices such as hymns sweetly purled on electronic bells, a more appropriate means of calling the people of God to the work of worship would be three sharp blasts from a factory whistle. That does not make such a proceeding an ideal liturgical form; but at least it would communicate the all-important sense of engagement in work. Islam is not unaware of the principle: from the minaret of the mosque the muezzin summons faithful Muslims to prayer. Pentecostals who yell for joy and Black Baptists who follow their own tradition of shouting "Alleluia!" and "Thank you, Jesus!" after the reading of the lesson are far closer to the spirit of liturgy than are those churches in which a reader in an academic robe concludes with the aspiration that God may add his blessing to the performance, as though one were expressing the hope that salt or pepper would be added to the soup.

The failure to recognize the all-important notion that liturgy is work, with the many dismal consequences of that failure, is no doubt historically connected with the Reformation disputes about the manner in which the

[1] *The Coming Reformation* (Philadelphia: Westminster Press, 1960), pp. 132 f.

Eucharist can be accounted a sacrifice. The subtle
theological questions need not be raised, since whether in
the Mass we offer God himself to God, as Catholic tradition insists, or offer him only a sacrifice of praise and
thanksgiving out of a contrite heart, which the Psalmist
assures us, he will not despise (Psalm 51:17) we do offer
God *something*, and anyone who thinks that that is not
work has much to learn about religion. To see churchgoing as joyful work does not in itself commit one, however, to this or that doctrine of the Eucharist. I suppose
even a Quaker or a Salvationist, neither of whom has the
Eucharist at all in any form, might in one way or another
account his worship a kind of work. The essential point is
that when we come to God, whether we think ourselves
empty-handed or making an oblation of Christ himself,
we are to work. Whatever we are doing, and whatever
happens to be our theological understanding of what is
called in Catholic tradition the holy sacrifice of the Mass,
we have not come all that way to church only to sit down
and listen to Bible readings that we could perfectly well
read in our armchairs at home, much less listen to theological boilerplate from the pulpit. Where the chief focus
is on the sermon, the people perish. In some exceptional
cases they may not perish of hunger, being fed with the
lively Word; but sooner or later they will perish from an
even greater need than the need for food. They will perish from being liturgically unemployed. The rate of liturgical unemployment in contemporary Christendom is
staggering.

Liturgy is in one respect like any other work: it requires a mixture of disciplined pattern and freedom to
move. All workers need both order and room to work. Too
restrictive rubrics leave no scope for personal choice of

collects, suffrages, and prayers for special needs. Such worship becomes at worst a repetitious rigmarole of flabby sentimentality and at best a visit to a well-stocked museum. It fails to engage people in work. Yet worship without any guidelines at all is even worse, producing all the frustration that attends anarchy. That, too, leads to idleness. When workers are cramped by stultifying conditions and hampered by excessive rules they are well on their way to slavery. The tedium they suffer precludes the exercise of any creative ability they might have had. Deprivation of orderly conditions, however, has an even more dismal result.

Within certain Protestant traditions is perpetuated a claim to be "nonliturgical" or "free." People within such traditions affect to have eliminated ritual and form. Some may even say they do not object to ritual form in other, that is, "liturgical" churches but that such ritual and form are alien to their own heritage. Nothing could be more conspicuously false. One might as well affirm that a man's suit has no shape unless it is London tailored or that a woman's clothes are shapeless because they were not styled in Paris. *All* clothes have shape. *Of course* so-called nonliturgical worship has form.

The old Quakers liked to think of themselves as the body of Christians who had more successfully than any other abolished form and ritual. Even Quaker worship of the old silent tradition has, however, both ritual and form. To sit on benches looking toward a facing bench of elders or officers of the society is form indeed, and to stand when moved by the Spirit is indeed ritual. From the standpoint of modern Pentecostalists the old Haverford Quaker tradition would seem outstandingly tied to ritual and constricted by form. Pentecostalists, however, have forms, too. One of my former students, a Minister of the Assembly of God, assures me that at Pentecostalist meetings participants whose manifestations do not conform to certain expected patterns are often held suspect by those who have for many years followed the Pentecostalist way. Presumably even rolling and howling are not to be performed entirely as one pleases. Sooner or later public opinion will favor certain ways of doing these acts and will frown on others. The floor will come to be recognized as the correct place for the rolling to be performed, and the nonconformist Pentecostalist who essays rolling on the radiators will invite disapproval as a show-off. It is bad form. He may even be accounted pneumatically deficient. If howling is standard procedure, one is not to howl indiscriminately; one must do one's howling according to certain principles.

In some so-called mainline bodies within the Reformation heritage, the situation has indeed been like that for a long time. Where plainsong would be accounted the most outrageous exhibition of an antiquated, Byzantine spirit, a vocal delivery having the most inflexible characteristics ever devised by the wit of man is imposed with obdurate rigor. Though the approved mode is definitely speech, not song, a singsong intonation pervades the entire performance. Vocatives like "O" rise in pitch and swell in volume in a great crescendo, while the divine names accompanying them, such as "Lord," "God," and the like, descend with a thud of despair like a family Bible thrown from the fifth-story window of a burning building to a waiting mattress below. No variation is permitted, no mitigation of the monotony is allowed. I have even heard a prayer, consisting almost exclusively of a discursive statement of gratitude for the gift of liturgical freedom, delivered with these excruciatingly unmodulated inflections, a sort of off-key *tonus peregrinus* in prose.

Good taste is by no means enough, however, as will be more fully considered in the next chapter. Worship that consists of liturgical pieces from the past, impeccably arranged and exquisitely rendered, can be just as much of a liturgical failure as the inflexible wails of a liturgical leader standing amidst his seated listeners. The sedentary position of the latter is very relevant to our subject. It was not accidentally adopted by champions of this school. It symbolized from the first the repudiation of the notion that liturgy is work. Puritan worship came to be a spectacle. It became the religious counterpart of bear-baiting, with the devil replacing the bear of more secular shows. It is notoriously difficult for spectators, when they know something is wrong with the spectacle, to specify precisely *what* is wrong. For that, one must be a participant; but not everyone is ready to tackle a bear or a devil. The Puritans came to account their clergy the professional devil-tamers. To paraphrase what Macaulay said of the Puritans' hostility to cruel sports, they were sometimes better pleased with their own pleasure than with the devil's discomfort.

The best conditions for liturgical participation are to be found when worship is pervaded by both discipline and freedom. There is no standard recipe for the mix; nor could there be. To ask what is the optimum proportion of the two ingredients is foolish. Fifty-fifty? Seventy-thirty? Of course not: neither freedom nor discipline can be measured. Both must be maximally present together, and worshipers must be trained over a long period to know how to use both.

In public worship in which an oral tradition prescribes

a dull structure that is accounted quasi-immutable, worship goes on Sunday after Sunday with a few arbitrary deviations introduced in a feeble, desperate, and spectacularly unsuccessful attempt to provide "variety." The leader, embarrassingly aware that the tedium of the same old string of liturgical items, the same dreary arrangement of hymns and homilies and prayers, is causing acute melancholy to take possession of his people, tries manfully to mend matters by enterprising attempts to deviate from the macabre array of verbal corpses hebdomadally inflicted upon the long-suffering flock. The latter have become so petrified by the habit of accepting the arrangement that they would never tolerate any formal deviation from it; nevertheless, thinks the leader, the anguish he knows they must be enduring is so great that they might be glad of a few asides which, though in fact well rehearsed, might look spontaneous, at least to hearts too grateful for relief from their unisong to allow their doubts to intrude. So, glancing up from the Bible from which he is reading a lesson, he boldly essays a few words, designed to seem extemporaneous, by way of commentary or exegesis. Or else, perhaps, he interpolates a few observations, to him ecstatic, to others comical or embarrassing, on the topical significance of the passage in hand.

The prayers follow the regular strain; but disastrously the leader tries his hand at an occasional incursion into what he takes to be originality. Perhaps, though it is Eastertide, he borrows, say, the collect for the first Sunday in Advent, for he is aware or has been told that it is beautiful. Yet it will not quite do. There are some features in it that do not wholly fit his own inchoate motif, and the language, of course, does not seem right, coming from him, who normally would no more talk like a collect than an insurance agent would talk like Hamlet. So he doctors it. "Almighty God, give us grace to come out of our darkness and pluck up courage to get into the light, now in this day and age in which Christ is always coming into our hearts to try to visit with us if we will let him, as we ought to do. Then, in the day of judgment, which as you know, Lord, is every day, may we feel a sense of leaping out into eternal life. For his sake we ask it, Lord. Amen." To anyone who knows and loves the collect, the effect is somewhat as though we were to touch up the Lord's Prayer with little topical flourishes and chatty asides to show that we were trying to avoid the charge of ritualism, and to keep the words from sounding monotonous through frequent repetition.

Such a leader is right in detecting that there is something far wrong with the liturgical heritage to which he and his flock have become so lugubriously accustomed. His mistake lies in supposing that the cure is a little dash of pretend spontaneity, a few uningenious departures from the weekly rigmarole. On the contrary, what is needed at that point is not less pattern but more. With a more carefully designed and intricate pattern, providing for variety throughout the liturgical year, the hearts and minds of the worshipers might overcome their depressing condition and be vivified by the expectation of a skillfully ordered novelty introduced into the woof of prayer. The skill of the historical liturgies is astounding. The pattern of the Christian Year, though it is not a liturgical panacea, does go a long way to preserve the conditions of liturgical health, and even a dull liturgy so ordered is not unexciting, if only the leader knows how to enunciate his mater-

nal tongue and is trained to refrain from attempts at gild-
ing the liturgical lily with his usually very ungolden
oratorical essays.   ·

Recognition of the principle that liturgy is work is the
surest safeguard against the extravagances that plague
worship, not least in times of liturgical renewal. Consider,
for instance, the kiss of peace. This had become so formalized as to be, in the old Roman rite, no more than a cautious inclination of the head of the giver over the left
shoulder of the receiver, with a formal bow before and
after the ritual gesture. One had to be something of a
liturgical scholar to know it symbolized a kiss of peace. In
the midst of the liturgical experiments of the Episcopal
Church in the early seventies, however, it sometimes acquired a character so startling that a timid recipient
might fear a fractured rib as the price of acceptance of a
demonstration of Christian love. There should be no need
to have to choose between a sickly, formalized ritual gesture, on the one hand, and, on the other, a wantonly demonstrative orgy. True, what would seem to an English-
man an outrageous display of warmth might well seem
unduly restrained to an American or a Greek. What is at
issue is not the amount of fervor but the appropriateness
for people who are at work. If a brotherly clasp of the
hand would seem right for a work-party, it will be right
for this work. If a more cuddly gesture would be natural
for the workers, the *pax* should take no less cuddly a form.
So long as we remember we are at work we shall never go
very far wrong. That provides as good a criterion for liturgical manners as genuine consideration for other people
provides the best guideline for good social manners. A
priest who slavishly looks up a Fortescue fares as badly as
would a hostess who relied solely on Amy Vanderbilt.

The same general principle provides the clue to why fussiness is as out of place at the altar as slovenliness. Fastidiousness and pedantry are all right for hobbies; but they are out of place at work. When we are indulging in our hobbies we have plenty of time. Our whole approach is intentionally unworkmanlike, and we can allow ourselves as many fads and foibles as we please. For pleasure is the whole point of a hobby. If you make ship models in your spare time, there is no end to the attention you may give detail. Against your competitor in the local club, who attends to detail only on the outside of the vessel, you may furnish the captain's cabin right down to having real Scotch in the millimeter-tall ship's decanter. Your model is in fact more perfect than any ship that ever sailed. All that is part of the fun. You can afford to do it because you are not really at work. By the same token, you can well afford to go around your mountain cabin unshaven and wearing pants torn at the knees and an old flannel shirt three sizes too large. That is part of the fun of having a lazy weekend. You would never dream of going like that to the office. Yet at the office you would avoid overdressing. You would dress for work; that is, you would dress, as you would do everything else, in whatever way was most conducive to efficient production. Lace cottas are bad liturgical taste, not because they look effeminate, and certainly not because some celebrated Benedictine liturgist has denounced them, but simply because they are not suitable work clothes. Wearing them is like wearing an opera hat to the office or dance pumps in the machine shop. Swimsuits and sequined evening gowns are both improper at a place of work, unless, of course, you happen to be, in the one case, a lifeguard and, in the other, a night-club singer. Yet so long as we would wear fine suit-

ings at the Supreme Court of the United States or at a
summit conference at Versailles, the use of damask at the
altar of God seems to me preferable to the prevailing
vogue of unbleached linen. Only priests who would go to
a White House conference in blue jeans should offer Mass
in jute.

Yet to know that liturgy is work is not enough. For to
work well we must know in what kind of work we are engaged. We must understand the nature of the business. So
before we leave this crucial topic let us try to clarify the
nature of the business we call liturgy.

The surest way of understanding and appreciating the
value of any kind of work is to ask, first of all, what difference it would make if it were not done. If no clothes
were manufactured by anybody, everybody would go
naked. Whether we think that important will depend on
how much, for one reason or another, we dislike or disap-
prove of nudity. Some, in moments of impatience, may
ask whether we really need the schools that cost taxpayers
such an enormous amount of money. Yet in spite of the
grievous shortcomings of our educational system, the alternative prospect of a totally unlettered population
would convince most people of the necessity of the work
the schools are commissioned to do. Then in what sense
can we claim that liturgy too is necessary work? What
does it do, the neglect of which would really dismay us?

The human psyche has a remarkable capacity both for
self-centeredness and for self-aggrandizement. Yet these
capacities are as nothing to our infinite psychological capacity for self-delusion. So skillful are we in deluding ourselves that we construct elaborate psychological devices
to protect our psyches from the danger of seeing ourselves
as we are. The protective mechanism is natural, instinc-

tive, and indispensable to our self-preservation, for without our delusions, especially our delusions of moral self-grandeur, we could not live, and if in some way we managed to do so we would be too discouraged at the sight of ourselves to be able to improve. We can no more be instantaneously cured of our psychological delusions than we can be so cured of obesity or hepatitis. The treatment involves long and hard work. Liturgy is the work of removing these psychological delusions. Wherever it fails it is well described as an opiate. The failure that Charles Kingsley saw in the English Church of his day was indeed well described by that charge, which he made against it before Marx ever used the phrase. The Church had become a psychological playground. It must be a workshop.

Worship is not, of course, the only way of mitigating our astounding delusions of moral self-grandeur. Our social instincts, which compel us even in childhood to take account of others, our peers as well as our parents, do help to remove some of the more ridiculous manifestations of our delusion. Without the process of coming to terms with these outside forces, children either would be autistic or else would remain such spoiled brats that they would be unable to endure one another at all. Nevertheless, that gregarious process, though it involves some painful exercises, yields only superficial results. The society it promotes is really at best only a vast network of mutual admiration groups. We tend to choose the companionship of others who for one psychological reason or another happen to be congenial to us; that is, they help us to keep our delusions from showing in public, so that we can give the illusion of humility without actually changing much of our cherished pride. Such companions are very precious to us because they perform a useful tranquilizing function. Our disquiet about our self-centeredness is lulled while at the same time we learn the art of pretending to a more reasonable assessment of ourselves than we have or would wish to attain. Success in this ruse varies, of course, as the psychiatrist learned who asked his patient whether he suffered from delusions of self-grandeur, only to receive the reply: "Oh no, as a matter of fact I think of myself as much less than I really am."

Most people, however, learn how to keep their delusions, like their private emotions, to themselves; at least they try not to let them conspicuously obtrude. That is largely indeed what civilization is: civilized people are those who have learned how to control themselves in such a way that life in human society becomes very much more agreeable than it would otherwise be and can eventually produce immensely refined ways of life that make gregariousness delightful. While it makes people often hide their strongest feelings, such as anger and sexual desire (which causes the thoughtless to decry it for fostering hypocrisy), and so pretend to an altruism they have by no means attained, the pretense does have some value besides making people more bearable to one another. For the very act of pretending gives people at least a glimpse of a vision of what life might be if only people really were morally tamed and not merely expert in the art of withdrawing from public view the ugly fangs of their self-centeredness and greed and lust.

Nevertheless, human civilization, even at the best, is mostly cosmetic, however pleasant and therapeutic a cosmetic it be. The great civilizations of the world, for all their splendor and their incalculable improvement of the human condition, are no more equipped to destroy our delusions than a beauty parlor is equipped to remove the blood ailment or hormone disorder that manifests itself in the acne the beauty parlor so cleverly disguises. For the radical excision of our delusions more arduous work is needed. We must do more than merely cover them up. We need to eradicate them, and that (despite the last and most desperate of our achievements in self-delusion, the one that makes us believe more perfect social cosmetics will do the trick) can be done only by recognizing a reality beyond the human race, the Eternal One whose creatures we are and on whom we depend for our existence. To labor not only to recognize the nature of our relation to that Being, but to learn to know and to love him above all else that falls or could ever fall within the ambit of our knowledge is the only way through which the radical excision of our self-delusion can take place. For our basic self-delusion springs from our natural tendency to deify ourselves. Our fellow creatures, far from removing it, often do nothing more for us than help us to engage in a conspiracy to strengthen and refine it.

The liturgy, in the light of these considerations, is the work of seeing ourselves in the right perspective in relation to the universe, but especially in the right perspective in relation to him whom we acclaim its source and its core. The work is arduous indeed; but to the extent that it is successful it is attended by unspeakable joy. Like all great work, including scientific work, it does not by any means consist in an endless procession of successes. On the contrary, the failures are conspicuous. One of the chief sources of our failure in this work is our tendency to cheat ourselves by trying to achieve the therapeutic result without acknowledging the extra-mental reality of the source whence only it could come. To overcome the human tendency to make ourselves believe that we hold the key to our own cure within ourselves, and that we therefore need only pretend to worship God, is our very last and wildest struggle to avoid the work we now know we have to do. Only those who have done at least a stint of such work can appreciate the difference that work makes to our human condition and how gruesome the world would be if liturgical unemployment were universal.

Chapter IV

THE RELEVANCE AND IRRELEVANCE OF BEAUTY

Wherever beauty has been quick in clay
Some effluence of it lives, a spirit dwells.
                    —John Masefield, *Sonnets*

THE function of aesthetic experience in religious worship is curiously ambivalent. On the one hand, the richest and noblest forms of liturgical worship, such as, say, the Liturgy of St. John Chrysostom and the Book of Common Prayer, and even indeed many hymns and canticles, are all, each in its own way, works of art. No religious commitment is needed to perceive their beauty. An atheist well grounded in historical and literary studies could aesthetically appreciate them. He might indeed enter a great church such as Amiens Cathedral or Santa Maria Maggiore and attend High Mass or Benediction there and be so entranced by the beauty of the ceremonial, the poetry of the language, and the joy of the music, to say nothing of the fine proportion and architectural splendor of the building, that his longing to return might very well be far greater than that of many sincere churchmen. The destruction of a great painting such as Murillo's "Immaculate Conception" might far more bitterly distress an atheist curator than perturb a Catholic saint.

Yet the devout person may indeed also very much appreciate the beauty of the worship, and usually does. He may well claim, moreover, to see a fundamental connection between the beauty and the nature of the ontological reality he calls God. He may deplore bald and uncouth forms of worship as peculiarly unworthy, and he may call certain "holy pictures" tawdry and certain hymns doggerel. No genuinely religious person, however, whatever his stance, would measure religious worth by the measuring-stick of art. The crucifix that has won a prize at an international art exhibit is not on that account, from a religious standpoint, a whit better than any other. It would certainly be far less prized than a cheap one that had been clutched in the hands of a dying saint. A drab church, or even a garish one, in which thousands of saintly men and women have opened their hearts to God in prayer will commend itself to religious-minded people far more than an architectural masterpiece overrun with hordes of art students and noisy tourists.

Various religious taboos suggest even a deep-seated suspicion of art as dangerous to devotion. Orthodox Judaism traditionally renounces all direct visual representation of religious ideas. Islam likewise, though it provides much scope for the embellishment of the mosque by floral and other conventional designs and has occasionally tolerated the representation of religious motifs, does not officially allow religious art that includes the human face or figure. The Greek Church, which on the Feast of Orthodoxy annually celebrates the restoration of the ikons it prizes, of which the people had been deprived during the Iconoclastic Controversy,[1] is restricted to two-dimensional art: pictures, yes; statues, no.

In what way, then, does religion look upon art and use it? How does art function in religion? While all liturgy is art, good or bad, it has always in it a special element of austerity and restraint. Plainsong, for instance, is peculiarly restrained. Therein lies much of its appeal. Without that austere restraint it would lose much of the religious aura that attends it, making it as recognizably religious as the *Marseillaise* is unmistakably martial and the Dead March funereal. Painting and sculpture, even in baroque churches, are not so flamboyant as they would be were the aim simply a particular kind of aesthetic experience. True, part of the restraint comes from the nature of art itself: the creativity of the artist, whatever his medium, and however he chooses to express his artistic impressions, entails an element of self-restraint. In liturgical art, however, there is an additional and different kind of restraining force, the special kind of restraint that is needed to take the artistic expression, which is an independent mode of experience and can be an end in itself, and offer it sacrificially to God.

Sacrifice is indeed the key to the relation between art and religion. The genuine artist, he who is more than a hack, engages in self-sacrifice in all his creative enterprise. I do not allude, of course, to sacrifice of money or leisure that artistic engagement may happen to require. That is

---

[1] A controversy about the veneration of ikons troubled the Greek Church from 725 to 842. For various reasons the emperors and others in high places opposed the use of ikons. Their opposition was extremely unpopular and widely resisted, especially by the monks. At last the persecution of ikon-users ceased and the popular triumph is commemorated in the Feast of Orthodoxy, held on the First Sunday in Lent in the Eastern Church.

merely incidental to the work of art. The basic sacrifice all
good art entails is the bending of the heart and mind to
what confronts the artist, which is intrinsically hard and
painful. We all enjoy letting our imagination run riot, and
the more imagination we have the more riotous we can let
it run; but that is no more art than bouncing a ball with a
tennis racquet is tennis. Genuine art, far from being a
flight from reality, entails the anguish of yielding to it in
order to present reality for the mind to appropriate. Liturgy presents the reality of God, as God confronts the
lively religious consciousness. That is an exercise that demands self-restraint, self-abnegation, self-sacrifice, and in
that sense liturgy may be called a form of art.

Liturgy also, however, transcends art in one respect,
and it is this respect that makes it suspect as a potential
danger to its own life. Even the most authentic artist, the
one who must engage in the most rigorous self-sacrifice in
his expression of nature as he finds it, is concerned only
with his own self-sacrifice. He is somewhat like an athlete
who is rightly concerned only about his own fitness, his
own current ability to do what he engages to do. That is
so because artists, like athletes, have no metaphysical concern about that which confronts them and demands their
submission, while genuine worshipers do. Worshipers do
not merely engage in self-restraint and self-sacrifice in
common with all artists and indeed all who seek to try to
appreciate any worthwhile form of art; they also engage
in contemplating the act of self-sacrifice that they find in
God, in the very heart of the divine creative act and
which, for Christians, expresses itself particularly in the
loving self-sacrifice and self-humiliation of God in his act
of becoming man "for us men and for our salvation." Artists, as such, engage in self-sacrifice because there is no

other way in which they can go about their work effectively. Worshipers engage in it because, at their best, they are enthralled by what they find in the self-sacrifice of God who contronts them in life. The difference between liturgy and art is no less striking than the affinity.

Such considerations are essential for making any attempt to find a criterion for liturgical taste. Take, for example, an over-fussiness in liturgy, which is not only peculiarly irritating to the average layman but a sure sign of liturgical ill-health. Fussiness is always, of course, a defect in any work of art, for it shows that the artist has not succeeded in getting to the heart of his problem and radically mastering it and has, instead, allowed himself to be sidetracked into intriguing but in the last resort profitless byways. He has been playing rather than working, and the result is irritating, much as is any sort of mind-wandering or "fiddling" that diverts attention from the business in hand. Fussiness in liturgy is all that; but it is very much more: it is a signal that the fuss-maker, at the point at which he makes the fuss, is failing to attend either to his own work or to God's. Not only is he not working; he is not listening, which means that even if he were working he would be missing the target.

When all that is said, however, liturgy may be treated as a special aesthetic form to which the ordinary rules of art apply. For instance, didacticism is lethal to every form of art. That is not to say that liturgy, like other forms of art, cannot accomplish any teaching mission. Of course it can and it must; but the teaching must be indirect. Liturgy must do its teaching as obliquely as does nature itself. Even the faintest suggestion of schoolmastering is ruinous to the rhythm of God, which has to flow unimpeded in, with, and through the whole liturgical movement.

That is why preaching, of whatever sort it may be, whether an exposition, a pleading, or a call, must be introduced as a break, an interruption. No doubt it is a most necessary and holy interruption; nevertheless it *is* an interruption. It is not the business of the hour but, rather, an interval, like the lunch period or the coffee break in an honest day's work at factory or office. It may be short or long, a homily or a full-scale sermon, depending on the needs and circumstances of the time and place, so long as it comes not as flowing with the liturgical tide but as a vessel sailing against the tide as she steers her course into dock. To say that is by no means to denigrate the importance of preaching; on the contrary, it is to give it its true place and the only one in which it can exercise its indispensable role of nourishing the life of the people of God.

The forms art takes vary immensely; but all art must have a form that exhibits one sort of meaning or another. The meaning may be relatively trivial and the form relatively simple, as in a pretty necklace for a little girl, or it may be much richer and more complex, as in a symphony or in an epic poem such as Dante's *Commedia*. Even a well-planned dinner menu has meaning, as indeed has a game of poker or a round of golf; but their meanings are restricted to a very limited range of human life and to a special and comparatively flat dimension within it. Great art lifts us beyond such cultural parochialism and opens up to us new vistas and new modes of being. Of no art can this be more true than it is of liturgy; yet the same principle holds here as elsewhere: the form, the structure, must be unimpeded, if the meaning is to be freely and clearly shown.

Many and pernicious, however, are the forces that conspire to inhibit the free flow of liturgical art. First and most obviously there is the bond of convention and habit. Nowhere does convention exercise a stronger psychological force than in attachment to an accepted religious ritual. The ritual may be good or bad, ancient or modern, ugly or beautiful. Such considerations seem to matter little. What grips the ritualist is not antiquity or beauty but his own sense of security in doing what in the past has been satisying to his psyche and which, therefore, he thinks he ought to be able to count upon to provide such satisfaction again. He wishes to be able to reproduce the experience that has proved psychologically valuable in the past and that, he hopes, will be equally valuable in the future. In self-defense he may invoke the artistic merit, the antiquity and historic continuity of the ritual he prefers, or, if that is impossible, he will uphold his ritual, if need be, on the ground that it *is* notably lacking in artistic merit. For since he will contend that art is irrelevant to religion and even an obstacle to religious commitment, he may argue that his adherence to the ritual he likes may be favored for its very lack of artistic worth. Once again, the reason matters little; what matters is that he can feel justified in pursuing his course. That course, however, is doomed to failure, because the spring of creativity has been dried up. Each attempt at re-enacting the once-living relationship produces the irritation and frustration of discovering that it is only the pale shadow of a remembered reality. The worshiper's devotion is like an old man's return to the arena of his youth in hope of recapturing the vitality and vigor he nostalgically associates with the scene.

Second, the turgidity of the emotions that permeate religious activities is often a considerable impediment to serious liturgical engagement. As the attention of the wor-

shiper is turned away from the sermon by the preacher's
voice, which is either too unctuous or too dry, too flippant
or too sanctimonious, too precious or too uncouth, so this
or that architectural feature, this or that kind of music,
even this or that scent, can alienate him from the whole liturgical enterprise. That is the point at which the discipline of acquiring the good taste that springs from a sense
of history can save the worshiper from being drowned in
a sea of his own emotions or trapped in the snare of his
own parochial prejudices. Nevertheless, having one's emotions restrained is by no means enough; they must be
profitably redirected. Mere erudition and taste, valuable
as they are, cannot by themselves produce the spark of
liturgical creativity.

Third, sheer laziness is a very real impediment to religious engagement. Various devices have been used in the
past to keep worshipers alert. Revivalistic preachers have
thumped and roared. Thumping and roaring does usually
keep people awake; but it tends to awaken them only to
the fact that the speaker is thumping and roaring. The
Catholic tradition provides a vast network of complicated
arrangements calculated to keep minds from wandering
and bodies from falling asleep; but that, too, is insufficient
for our purpose. Saying aloud one *Our Father* and ten
Hail Marys for every decade of the rosary is incompatible
with sleep; but it is very compatible with calculating
Fleet Filly's chances in the horse race. Following the complicated rubrics of a solemn pontifical High Mass might
well keep one's mind from wandering off to such mundan-
ities; but they might nevertheless do no more than fill it
with futile preoccupations such as noting that the mini-
mal bow was made where the rubrics prescribe the medial
one or that the bishop, on removing his mitre, adjusted his
hair. All the ingenious devices we employ to keep people's

attention do just that. They keep people's attention. They may do nothing to promote creativity. They keep us awake; they do not by any means necessarily awaken us to new liturgical life. Fasting, now soft-pedaled in the Catholic tradition that made so much of it in the past, was probably often helpful in bestirring sluggish imaginations. The great seventeenth-century Bishop Lancelot Andrewes once remarked that it is hard work preaching to a pound of steak and a pint of beer. Not only is a full stomach a deterrent to lively cerebral activity; it diminishes the imaginative capacity on which the beginnings of religious insight so much depend. Yet fasting, too, is certainly no guarantee of religious commitment or even of liturgical renewal. Chastity was at one time accounted helpful in producing religious insight, and I do not think our forefathers were by any means wrong in their high assessment of its power. Yet it is well known that sexual deprivation can also produce nothing more fruitful than frustration. Like everything else that our forefathers rightly perceived to be capable of producing creative results, it assuredly cannot guarantee them.

Our forefathers were more perspicacious, however, when they noticed, as some of them did, that fasting, chastity, and other ascetic disciplines, though none of them is a royal road to religious awakening, can all be *used* as possible aids for those who, through some other less conventional and stereotyped agency, have already found the way to God. When you have fallen in love you will delight in new words, new gestures, new discoveries that enable you to express that love more vividly and with greater vitality and precision; but none of these words or gestures or discoveries will in itself *cause* you to fall in love. That is what many people unversed in the history of religion and, much worse, only very superficially touched

by the impact of the Breath of God, are only just beginning to learn.

The first lesson to be learned about liturgical art is that it
is what you do when you have fallen in love with God,
not what you do in hope of falling in love with him. Once
you know that, you will never be troubled by a fear of
beauty or a suspicion of art. If you have not yet fallen in
love with God, beauty may well indeed prove a hindrance
and art a snare.

What, then, is the falling in love that is a precondition
of liturgical art, and how is it accomplished? While the
full answer to that question lies beyond the scope of our
topic, a few points may usefully be made. Setting aside all
theological considerations about grace and all the metaphysical conundrums attending such inquiries, we must
notice that what brings the God-dimension into one's life is
never a liturgical exercise, of either the Quaker or the
Roman Catholic, the Baptist or the Greek Orthodox sort;
it is always a set of circumstances in human life and one's
own response to that set of circumstances. The anguish of
these circumstances, the hunger for a way out to victory
over them, a longing for "something better": these are the
stuff out of which emerges the Great Awakening of the
human soul. Nevertheless, when a human being who has
been to the depths of human despair and has tasted the
bitterest pangs of human hunger for a better way is confronted with the rhythm of God, for example in the Holy
Sacrifice, the Eucharistic Feast, he knows and can never
again forget what falling in love with God means. If, being
less fortunate, he is able to hear only distant liturgical
echoes of that central act of Christian joy, he may well find
even in these mere echoes a wistful enchantment and a
much-sought peace.

Chapter V

PRINCIPLES OF LITURGICAL CHANGE

> There is danger in reckless change; but greater
> danger in blind conservatism.
> —Henry George, *Social Problems*

THAT liturgical changes ought sometimes to be made follows from what we have seen of the nature of liturgy if
not from the general considerations about the old and the
new that were advanced at the outset. Liturgy is not a
museum treasure but a growing and living reality. Nothing in religion is more soul-destroying than obstinate liturgical ideophobia. To say that is to say much, for religion,
though sometimes provocative of political revolution, is
also the most notoriously conservative of all societal
forces. We saw also at the outset that obstinate resistance
to all liturgical reform never depends on antiquity. It is
governed solely by a stupidity not infrequently seasoned
with malice. The stupidity is at least as readily found in
new ecclesiastical societies as in old ones.

Usages such as the individual communion tumbler,
which did not come into general use in Protestant worship

till about World War I, was by the time of World War II
more deeply entrenched than if it had been specifically
prescribed in the Didache. In Scottish Presbyterian worship, standing prevailed as the posture for prayer right
down to the middle of the nineteenth century, when improved communication and transportation by railroad
brought increasing influence from the fashionable nonconformist churches in London; but by the end of the
century sitting at prayer had become so sanctified by use
that it was as if it had been ordained on Sinai. To religious literalists, Muslim or Catholic, Jewish or Hindu,
Mormon or Sikh, not even social institutions like caste,
nor even dietary laws like the Jewish proscription against
eating meat and dairy produce at the same meal, are accounted more inviolable than is liturgical utterance and
ritual act.

Paradoxically, however, the apostles of reckless change
are much more like these blind conservatives than they
commonly seem. Both alike fail to understand that liturgy, like language, is a living entity and that, as with all
living entities, its sustenance and its power are inseparable from its growth. The blind conservative forgets this
because he fails to see that liturgy must bear fruit; the
apostles of reckless change forget it because they fail to
understand that liturgy must have roots and that, if you
cut these roots, it will wither and die an undignified
death.

I have likened the growth of liturgy to the growth of
language. The analogy is worth pursuing. The greatest
and most ductile of modern languages, those that are best
fitted for the expression of subtle thoughts and neat dis-
tinctions as well as for lyrical enjoyment and the exercise
of rhetorical power, are those that have been able to nour-

ish their own roots while assimilating a variety of enriching influences.

French is a good example. There we may more easily see the principle than we could in our own language, which is often too close to us. Theoretically, if anything could have stultified and petrified the French language, its formalization centuries ago by the French Academy should have done so. Yet it developed into one of the richest media in the history of mankind, expressive and elegant as a means of diplomatic communication and polite converse as well as a ductile instrument for the expression of precise and analytical thought. Moreover, by adapting itself to its environment with characteristically Gallic realism, it has been able to extend itself endlessly without infidelity to its own genius. It has done so, for example, by an infinite openness to new words without ever putting the rhythm of its own life in jeopardy. Beyond the exclusive rigor of the Academy's *grammaire* and *dictionnaire* it has developed a vast vocabulary of idiomatic usage, including a slang and a *langage populaire* pungent enough to penetrate to the heart of the French language yet so volatile and ephemeral that unless you have been living in Paris in the last year or two your slang may sound as antique as if you had learned it from a dictionary of *argot* published about the time of the Franco-Prussian War.

The secret should be instructive to liturgists. French assimilates alien elements only after the strictest and most formal procedures of linguistic naturalization. It takes in words from languages as diverse as English and Chinese, Arabic and Greek; but all must pass through the purifying Gallic fire. So the English mildew must become *mildiou* and "cowboy" is pronounced as though written *kovboua*. There was a time when, in fashionable circles in the *seiz-*

ième, one might hear the imported English tea-hour called *le five-o'clock* and pronounced, of course, *feevo-cloc.* I once personally had to admit defeat when a waiter asked me at breakfast if I wanted some *kakères-oua.* I fancied it might be a Moroccan import. It turned out to be nothing more exotic than Quaker Oats. The French know well the principle so successfully used in India for thousands of years in maintaining the identity of the religion of the Indus Valley that we Westerners call Hinduism. That remarkable religion has shown itself to be infinitely open to new ideas while rigorously molding them to its own peculiar genius and distinctive form. When Buddhism emerged in India half a millennium before the birth of Christ, it must have looked to many of its followers as though it would eventually supplant its Hindu parent. The opposite happened. Its Hindu parent took the central themes of Buddhism (which were of course deeply rooted in various strains of early Hindu thought and its presuppositions), skillfully adapted them, and poured them into the mainstream of its own life. Buddhism, though it spread in its Mahayana form with remarkable success in other lands, notably China and Japan, lost ground in the land of its origin to such an extent that, except for Ceylon, it has virtually died out. To modern Hindus it seems at best unnecessary and at worst *de trop.*

Christianity has by no means lacked such adaptive skill. It used it from the first, in its early encounters with the Gentile world, notably in its attitude to Gnosticism. The skill such achievements require can hardly be overestimated. They demand not only delicate perceptivity, extraordinary patience, and an uncanny sensitivity to the deepest needs of men and women, but a farsightedness that is unusual in any people and that all the conditions of occidental life conspire to make extremely rare in the West today. The adaptation of ancient Christian liturgical documents and their transmission as they have come alive in the day-to-day worship of the Church from century to century has reflected that great Christian skill and insight. Contemporary efforts at liturgical revision are not without either the skill or the insight, and there is certainly more liturgical erudition than was ever readily attainable in earlier times. Nor should we neglect to recognize the special difficulties that modern revisers face and how easy it is to criticize the results they offer. Nevertheless, in attacking their difficult task they have not always exhibited the kind of wisdom that throughout the ages has so much helped to enrich our Christian inheritance.

The Anglican task has its own particular difficulties and its own special advantages. Anglicans, who naturally know and love the Book of Common Prayer better than others are likely to know or to love it, are as painfully aware of its shortcomings as they are joyously conscious of its splendors. Neither the shortcomings nor the splendors are or could be those of the Roman Missal or the Liturgy of St. James. The revision of the Book of Common Prayer at this point in history requires a skill Cranmer himself might have envied. Not even the least learned among Anglican worshipers is wholly insensitive to the dangers attending the enterprise of updating their beloved book. They are often, however, unable to put into words their misgivings and their malaise. The project of revision seems laudable. The Prayer Book has already undergone various changes in the course of its history and travels through the expanding Anglican Communion. These show that changes *can* be felicitous. Surely few can regret, for instance, the American preference for "devoutly kneeling" over the English "meekly kneeling upon your knees" of the 1662 Book, which might provoke unprofitable speculations about how else one could go about kneeling.

When the Standing Liturgical Commission of the Episcopal Church considered the need for further improvements, the result, as it eventually appeared in *Services for Trial Use*, was not widely acclaimed, even after it had received fair trial. Few, surely, could see *no* good in it; but it brought conspicuously little joy even to those who in principle eagerly welcomed its advent. The general feeling seems to have been a vague sense of having been undefinably let down. After all the hard work the commission put into their task, and despite the liturgical learning they brought to it, nobody seemed particularly well pleased and many were deeply hurt and infinitely grieved.

Let us inspect a random example: the Invitation addressed by the priest to the people in which he asks them to join him in the General Confession in preparation for the momentous act in which they are about to engage. The commission had admitted, in their preparatory studies, that they could think of no improvement over the existing wording except that something should perhaps be done with the phrase "to your comfort," which they dubbed "obsolescent." Their misgivings about it were based on considerations that could have troubled only the learned. The average person, even the average well-educated person, could not have shared their perplexities, which sprang from the fact that since the sixteenth century the word "comfort" has undergone a change of meaning. Then it had conveyed the notion of invigoration and encouragement; now it suggests only solace. What to do?

They toyed with the notion of substituting something such as "to sustain and strengthen you." [1]

In the long run, however, two alternatives were offered in *Services for Trial Use*. One was to omit the Invitation entirely. The other, more traditionalist, alternative was to eliminate only the whole phrase "and take this holy Sacrament to your comfort," putting nothing in its place at all. True, the meaning of the word has changed over the course of the centuries. True, too, that the Church must often give the faithful, in Trevor Huddleston's memorable phrase, "naught for your comfort." Nevertheless, we may well ask whether the impoverishment of meaning the revisers had so diligently considered really justifies total excision. The less philologically learned account the loss a personal deprivation, an incomprehensible attack on their devotional custom and inclination. The more erudite, meanwhile, being secure in their learning, could not possibly be in any way misguided by the inclusion of the beloved phrase that was dropped out. Who, then, is the beneficiary of the commission's great expenditure of energy and skill? Was not a gnat strained out and a camel swallowed?

Casual worshipers might not even notice such liturgical *tours de passe-passe*. Not even the most perfunctory worshiper however, could fail to observe that to the priest's ancient greeting, "The Lord be with you," which would be recognizable even in its Latin form by any well-read Jew or Muslim, he was expected, in the "Second Service," to respond with that extraordinarily pedestrian, anticlimactic "And also with you." Why, he may well wonder, have Rome and Canterbury seemingly conspired against him to

[1] *Prayer Book Studies*, IV (New York: The Church Pension Fund, 1953), p. 131.

deprive him of the second half of the most hallowed inter-
change in the history of Christian worship while permit-
ting him the first? None can doubt that the beautiful salutation "The Lord be with you" is, in its English form,
almost as antique as "Prithee, lend me your ears." But
anybody who could enjoy a Shakespeare play can understand that phrase without a dictionary, and even among
those who could not tolerate Shakespeare surely none
would accept without astonishment a response such as
"We're listening, kid." If we are to expect congregations
to say, "And also with you" without a vast wincing of the
People of God, we must first require the priest to say
something equally drab to match the response and make
it seem proper, such as "I hope the Lord will visit with
you soon, friends." Such an outright paraphrase of both
parts of the beloved salutation, assuring us the dreariest
language the wit of man could devise, would be less of a
literary and liturgical gaffe. "And also with you" after "The
Lord be with you" demands a Bible to match, with open-
ers such as "And it came to pass that the Lord was real
mad."

Can it be improper, then, to ask what such proposed
changes could possibly do for anyone, young or old,
learned or simple, rich or poor? The phrase in the Nicene
Creed, "all things visible and invisible," is no doubt more
trying to unbaptized Gentile teenagers than is "coffee
and doughnuts"; nevertheless, would these important re-
cipients of our missionary enterprise be greatly enlightened by "all things seen and unseen"? Plainly not. Not in
the words but in the concepts is the root of the difficulty
to be found. The quest for plain Saxon speech is eminently laudable in itself, and were it also to achieve the
clarification of even one troubled mind, no one need feel

called upon to bear with the Latinity of even so hallowed a phrase. But since we are expected to cope with such metaphysical mouthfuls as "eternally begotten of the Father" and "begotten, not made, one in Being with the Father" (the retention of which was approved in the same proposed revision), one wonders which of us might be enlightened by calling the invisible the unseen. I know high school dropouts whom "visible and invisible" would not baffle, and I also know some distinguished chemists and biologists who would scream with puzzlement at "eternally begotten of the Father." Whom, then, do such typical changes serve?

Again, there is something to be said (though some of us much doubt it) for the notion that many people are irked by the quaint "Thou" and "Thee" used in address to God. Yet if we can contend with "compassed us about with so great a cloud of witnesses," which *Services for Trial Use* and *Authorized Services* 1973 offer us under the bold head "Contemporary Wording," might not we cope with "Thou" as the intimate form of address by the creature to his Creator? A student who has mastered calculus cannot fairly plead that the multiplication table is beyond his mathematical powers. "Thou" in fact draws loving hearts closer to their Saviour while "You" distances them. After all, one *could* update *Kyrie eleison* by translating it "Have mercy, Sir," which is a perfectly legitimate rendering with a much more contemporary air about it than has "compassed us about with so great a cloud of witnesses." Many of us think that "You" has a similar effect. French Protestants have for long understood that. They have traditionally asked, in the Lord's Prayer, "*Que* ton *règne vienne*," while their Catholic brethren have commonly prayed instead, "*Que* votre *règne arrive*." I happen to be among those who think the French Protestant usage is at this point to be preferred; but in any case we must ask again: For whom are such changes really profitable?

There is, indeed, no way in which the Book of Common Prayer can be turned into a twentieth-century book, for it was never a sixteenth- or a seventeenth-century one. As the editor of a scholarly analysis of the sources of the Prayer Book wrote of it in 1847, it

is no production of modern times, and refuses to be interpreted on modern principles, and by modern theories. Its roots strike deep into the Liturgies of far-distant Patriarchates of the early Church, and how much deeper, it is impossible to ascertain. From them it has derived its form and character; to them it is indebted for its peculiar construction; and by them alone can its true nature be tried and known. How entirely this essential principle of interpretation was lost sight of by many so-called *Reformers* of the Liturgy, is shewn by the melancholy proposals of alteration which they made; for, in not a few cases, what they imagined to be defects or vain repetitions, were component parts of every existing ancient Liturgy.[2]

The principle of cohesion is difficult enough for those who are called to undertake the revision of Anglican liturgy. Roman liturgists have an added problem when they are expected to mix Latin with the vernacular. What is now commonly called the traditional Roman Mass was in use throughout the world wherever the Latin rite prevailed from 1570 till November 26, 1969, when Paul VI is-

---

[2] Henry Bailey, *Rituale Anglo-Catholicum* (London: John W. Parker, 1847), Preface, pp. xx f. He quotes Pearson, *Concio I ad Clerum*, Vol. II, p. 13, ed. Oxon: "Multa . . . novatoribus non placent; et ea quidem plerumque quae optima, quia sunt antiquissima." The writer, through copious citations from patristic sources, Greek and Latin, exhibits the cohesiveness of the Prayer Book as well as its historic continuity.

sued an allocution calling attention to changes about to
be made. The Roman Mass had, of course, also a more ancient ancestry with roots in the Gregorian, Gelasian, and
Leonine sacramentaries. If, being familiar with the traditional Roman Mass, we were to go back in our imagination to, say, the seventh century, and visit a papal celebration as described in the *Ordo Romanus Primus*, we should
certainly find some of the customs, trappings, and dress
unfamiliar; nevertheless, we could easily enough recognize the rhythm. There could be little doubt in our minds
that we were looking at a celebration of the Latin Mass.

The *Kyrie* would be sung near the beginning, in Greek
as it is being sung thirteen hundred years later in St. Pat-
rick's, New York. The Pope would then turn to the people
and begin the *Gloria in excelsis* in Latin and immediately
turn eastward till the choir had finished singing it. Origi-
nally that hymn was sung in Greek too and when it was
introduced into Rome in the fifth century it was sung on
Christmas night only, though till about the eleventh
century only bishops were allowed to use it. Since the
Mass we were attending would be a papal one, the *Gloria*
would be included, and it would be in its normal
"Roman" place. Then the collect, lessons, Gospel, Creed
would follow, so that throughout the whole of the pro-
anaphora a Roman Catholic in the year 1968 would have
had the feeling of being at a Latin Mass which, though
celebrated according to a different usage from the one to
which he was accustomed, would seem less unfamiliar
than, say, the twentieth-century Ruthenian or Greek
Uniate rite. The rhythm would be similar, and of course,
though Latin has changed in the course of thirteen centuries, the language would provide a vital bond of union.
The Mass would have been changed; but the changes that

occurred would seem like the changes that occur in a living organism such as the human body. If you have been seeing a person daily over the course of many years you do not notice the changes that are imperceptibly overtaking all of us all the time. If, however, you have not seen the person for twenty or thirty years you may be slightly shocked; nevertheless, such changes as occur in the living body of a friend you deeply love do not prevent your recognizing him even in such circumstances, and you are likely to love your friend all the more for having survived them.

The changes that have taken place in Roman Catholic usage since 1969 are of another order. Extremists such as Father Wathen have bitterly attacked them.[3] The language of some such antagonists sometimes suggests a literalistic outlook that makes their sense of theological betrayal very understandable. Such extreme positions need not concern us here. Nevertheless, one must surely sympathize with those many Roman Catholics who feel their birthright has been sold for a mess of very tasteless pottage. On the pretext of making the liturgy more accessible to the people, especially young people (though these are often better able to appreciate the poetry of the Mass than were some of their elders), the Roman Mass has been shorn of its haunting power because deprived of its literary cohesion.

Even if one could approve the enterprise in principle, one would still have to ask about the price. Let us take a random example. For Easter morn the lovely post-communion collect is preserved: "Spiritum nobis, Domine, tuae caritatis infunde: ut quos sacramentis pas-

[3] James F. Wathen, O.S.J., *The Great Sacrilege* (Rockford, Ill.: Tan Books, 1971).

chalibus satiasti, tua facias pietate concordes. Per Dominum nostrum Jesum Christum filium tuum, qui tecum vivit et regnat in unitate ejusdem." True, fifty years ago almost any well-educated Protestant could have construed such easy Latin. Today, however, when Latin is as rare a tongue as Sanskrit and perhaps sometimes even rarer, since some colleges that no longer teach Latin are reportedly teaching Sanskrit, the language barrier for the majority of people is indeed great. It is not wholly insuperable, of course, for Jews have solved their similar problem by the institution of Hebrew schools attached to even Reform synagogues. Still, we must not pretend the problem does not exist. Nevertheless, we must ask whether those for whom it does exist can fare better with the following adventure in an unknown tongue. It represents the eleventh-century Sequence of the Mass, *Victimae Paschali*:

Christians, to the Paschal victim
> Offer your thankful praises.
A lamb the sheep redeemeth: Christ, who only is sinless,
> Reconcileth sinners to the Father.
Death and life have contended in that combat stupendous:
> The Prince of life, who died, reigns immortal.

Speak, Mary, declaring,
> What thou sawest, wayfaring.

Surely no one could find such language easy unless he were a learned theologian who had made a lifelong hobby of translating theological propositions into the jargon of a government department. My complaint is not, however, at the stylistic poverty. Liturgical Latin was never by any means always a literary joy. My complaint is that nobody

in the world could possibly find any advantage in having
such difficult and complex theological concepts expressed
in a ludicrously prosy non-English whose cumbersome
opacity would have turned off every intelligent saint in
the Roman calendar and could do nothing but trouble the
minds and sadden the hearts of the saints of tomorrow.

In liturgical reform, the principle of cohesion matches
in importance even theological fidelity, for it is the vehicle by which the theology must be conveyed. Bad liturgical style can diminish and even corrupt good theology as
surely as a bad preacher can make the most faultless, ex-
citing, and beautiful Christian teaching sound dull. Not
for nothing has it been said that while an actor can make
trivial words sound the most important in the world, a
clergyman can make the most important words in the
world sound trivial. The task of revising the liturgy is indeed formidable, for it demands not only liturgical learning, which is learning of a very technical and specialized
kind, but a unique combination of theological acumen
and literary discrimination and power. Among the moral
qualities it demands, not least vital is the self-discipline
to ask at every point, "Is a change really necessary?" and
the honesty to say, "No," when that is the only correct
answer.

Enthusiasts for liturgical reform are often troubled
about communication problems that are more in their
own minds than in anyone else's. The average man-in-
the-pew does indeed have difficulties; but they are seldom
the difficulties the liturgical revisers try to treat. As with
the Bible, the problems are more with concepts than with
words. We need only meager instruction to make us
understand that "Ghost" is just a beautifully hallowed

English archaism for "Spirit" and one that helps us to enter into that historic dimension apart from which the notion of the Church is meaningless. We need years of intensive training, however, to understand why the Church need talk of a Third Person of the Trinity at all, and why indeed we need a trinitarian formulation of our faith. Liturgical scholars are more apt than other people to be trapped into thinking that "true God from true God" is going to be more intelligible to the average worshiper than is "Very God of Very God." In fact it is like telling a Confucian he need not be troubled by the Christian notion that God is omniscient, because the word means simply that God is all-knowing, or trying to help me to understand legal terminology by ceasing to use the Latin term *ultra vires* and offering me instead an English alternative: "beyond men." The task for liturgists is far more difficult, and its fulfillment will include a much greater sense of respect for the contemporary mind.

Though the language of Cranmer that Anglicans inherit in the Prayer Book is much closer to our own than is Chaucer's, the average educated person of English speech who has no particular Christian concern is likely to make more of Chaucer than he is of Cranmer. The reason is plain: Chaucer's thoughts are not usually so alien to such a person as are the theological concepts of the Bible and the Prayer Book. If the modern worshiper is to learn how to use the liturgy intelligently and profitably, he will learn it through commentary and instruction rather than through the kind of changes we have been discussing.

In our first chapter we mentioned a few examples of commendable changes in the liturgy, and in the present one we have enunciated one principle for determining

what we should and what we should not commend: the
principle of cohesion. I think we should in any case never
twist the order or alter the phrasing without an over-
whelmingly compelling reason. It is generally better, I believe, to live with what we have than to gain a technical
improvement at the cost of inducing sorrow and confusion
among those who love their Anglican heritage while
doing nothing to mitigate the incomprehension and
disdain of those outside. I am not even sure that the obviously defensible change to "Drink this, all of you," for
"Drink ye all of this" is to be preferred to preserving the
traditional form and at the same time giving priests a
better training in the art of speech. Nevertheless, when all
that is said, we must be very open to every possibility of
enhancement of our liturgical inheritance.

The response after the Gospel in the Scottish Liturgy
could hardly be a diminishment; nor could it go against
the principle of cohesion: instead of "Praise be to thee, O
Lord" it has "Thanks be to thee, O Lord, for this thy glorious Gospel." The litaneutical form of intercession is so ancient, so moving, and so abundantly adapted to the needs
of the people in every age that a place should certainly be
found for it. I think the use of an English rendering of the
Domine, non sum dignus[4] immediately before the communion of the faithful is such a help to the devotion of
many people that much is to be said for its recognition as
at least an optional addition. People are not nearly so
much distressed by salutary additions as they are by omis-
sions, even those for which the most eminently sound ar-
guments may be invoked. Personally I think the restora-

---

[4] "Lord, I am not worthy that thou shouldest come under my roof:
say but the word and my soul shall be healed" (cf. Matthew 8:8).

tion of the Greek form *Kyrie eleison* is a defensible change, if only because, in an age that is so sadly bereft of historical awareness, it neatly and, if I may so speak, painlessly brings into focus the continuity of the Church's life. To pretend that it is too difficult, too learned, for the ordinary worshiper is absurd. The ordinary worshiper has been for centuries shouting hosannas and alleluias and amens, without usually even knowing that he was talking Hebrew, so the *Kyrie* should not daunt him. The view that opportunity should be provided for extempore prayer for the priest, and for anyone else who wishes to offer it, is surely beyond question, as is also the need for a fuller use of liturgical silence.

That the extension of the *pax* to the whole congregation should prove so contentious in many parishes seems at first sight somewhat shocking. Are Christians afraid or resentful of greeting one another with an embrace expressive of the *agapē* without which we are, as St. Paul warns us, no more than tinkling cymbals? The distaste may arise from the unfortunate fact that the *pax* is often given either so gingerly or so exuberantly as to convey the impression of phoniness. Sometimes we find ourselves treated as though we were lepers being approached by a timid medical missionary who had belatedly summoned up courage to enter the island colony but at the last minute had inclinations to retreat, yet wished not to offend the lepers. On other occasions we are alarmed by an onslaught such that we fear the fracture of our ribs. I see nothing to be desired in either of these extremes. Mature Christian love is neither so exuberant nor so timid as to produce such dispiriting results. To receive the kiss of peace from such a mature Christian is to know what joy there is in that disci-

pline of oneself and overflowing compassion to others, the
lack of either of which suffocates the Christian soul. Better a restrained handshake that conveys *agapē* than a
bear hug that only too abundantly expresses nothing more
than vulgar camaraderie. Yet that is by no means to dis-
parage more demonstrative greetings when occasion calls
for them. Nor must we ever forget the immense loneliness
that many people suffer in contemporary metropolitan
life, which may be healed by the touch of a genuinely
concerned fellow member of the Body of Christ.

I am inclined to the view that behind the more reckless
programs of liturgical change lie a curious and depressing
combination of technical snobbery, on the one hand, and,
on the other, a capitulation to the anti-intellectualism in
the Church that is one of the most potent factors in alienating intelligent people from it. Millions of people who
are more repelled by the obvious dedication of church
people to the most virulent forms of that anti-
intellectualism and who on that account alone would
never think of attending anything churchy other than a
funeral or a wedding are, of course, the very people who
could, with a minimum of explanation, most readily appreciate the splendor of the Church's liturgical symbolism.
Yet too often the Church gives the impression of being fe-
verishly engaged in denuding the liturgy of the very
beauty that might attract them while at the same time
saddening the hearts of her own children. Well might we
ask once again: Whom, then, is she hoping to please? By
now, however, that has become a question that silence answers better than speech.

There is much in the liturgy that cannot be changed
without jeopardizing the whole life of the Church. There
are also, however, some things in it that should be

changed and that can be changed within the rhythm of God. What is needed, and is by no means readily come by, is what Niebuhr, in his now famous prayer, called the "wisdom to distinguish the one from the other." [5]

[5] Reinhold Niebuhr composed the prayer ("O God, give us serenity to accept what cannot be changed, courage to change what should be changed, and wisdom to distinguish the one from the other") in 1934, and he used it in the little church near his summer home in Heath, Massachusetts. See June Bingham, *Courage to Change* (New York: Charles Scribner's Sons, 1961), p. iii. It is a prayer that unmistakably carries the divine rhythm.

Chapter VI

LITURGY, LAUGHTER, AND LOVE

You could read Kant by yourself if you wanted;
but you must share a joke with someone else.
— Robert Louis Stevenson, *Virginibus
Puerisque*

BY far the worst disaster that can befall a Christian parish
is the loss of love. So long as liturgy expresses Christian
love it can sustain almost any other kind of impoverishment. No other blow to it is mortal. The lovelessness that
kills a parish is easily detectable even in the early stages
of the disease. No great liturgical learning is needed to
discern it. Indeed, millions lacking the benefit of such
training have seen it in church after church and, sad or
sullen, have simply walked away. Nobody enjoys an
evening, let alone a morning, in a loveless household, least
of all in a household that calls itself the Household of
Faith.

Let us be cautious, however, in what we take lovelessness to be. People may fight like cat and dog yet be full of
authentic love. They may never have a cross word and be
as loveless as a polar icecap. Lovelessness is not at all to

be identified with lack of exuberance; nor is it to be pro-
moted by injunctions to engage in uninhibited howls of
friendliness or cuddly embrace. It is as compatible with
such ostentatious cheeriness as it is with sour-faced
gloom. A congregation infected by it not only has that
firm grasp of the nonessentials that has turned millions
away running and left dozens of unsmiling neurotics behind; it has lost the power to appropriate the means of
salvation. Only those who have been forgiven can laugh
at themselves, for only they have learned to love. One has
the impression, when one strays into a parish at worship,
a parish that is truly alive in Christ, that the people, for
all their idiosyncrasies, their personal tragedies and their
peculiar neuroses, are gently laughing at themselves.

The health of a parish is reflected in its prevailing sense
of mirth. To say of a parish that it is staid or set in its
ways is not a mild reproach, like calling its rood screen
heavy or its reredos cold. It is the worst charge you can
make, far worse than calling it crazy or silly or wild. The
latter is to the former what, in criminal law, a traffic viola-
tion is to first-degree murder. Only the hopelessly blind
will confuse quiet Christian restraint with spiritual de-
crepitude, or cheery-cherry noisomeness with Christian
life. Discriminating Christians soon learn that Christian
mirth is measured not in decibels but in the love that
finds God in the face of a brother pilgrim. Mirth is completely indispensable to Christian health. Its function in
the Church at prayer is infinitely more important than im-
peccable liturgical taste.

There is profound truth in a poem of the era of World
War I that concludes with a fanciful image: the creation
of ducks. God, having finished making the stars, the big
things in the universe, turned to the making of little

things, like daisies and ducks. Ducks were necessary, lest
men and women should become so glum, so forgetful of
God as to take even themselves seriously. Finally, when
God looked down into the ducks' bright eyes he smiled
and may even be still laughing at the funny "quack"
ducks make.[1] That is the kind of pointer to God's nature
that we need if we are to capture the mirth of Christian
maturity. We must learn to let such mirth transform us in
our worship, killing our legalisms and literalisms by its
power. Worship that so transforms us is never "said"; even
when there is not a note of music in it, it is always "sung."
That is to say, it will have flown out and away from the
flat and artificial dimension in which so much of our lives
are spent, wafting its way on the wings of the poetry of
God. It is a low-keyed laughter, the laughter of deep humility, the laughter issuing from the joy of Christian
prayer. There is no other mirth quite like it, and its presence attests the authenticity of the work of the people of
God.

However grand our liturgy, however subtle and delicate the choice of word and action, however impressive
the historical and theological learning that has gone into
every phrase, it will be a museum piece unless it reflects
the gentle mirth that is the fruit of active Christian love.
We who enjoy the privilege of inheriting ancient Catholic
usage in all its rich splendor should be especially mindful
of the source whence flows its spiritual power. When our
heritage seems to have become arthritic, the remedy is
not to be found in Rock Masses and Benediction with
Bagpipes (useful as occasional such experiments may
be), but in the recapture of that gentle joy that flows

[1] Cf. F. W. Harvey, "Ducks," in *Poems of Today: Second Series* (London: Sidgwick and Jackson, 1922), pp. 47 f.

from living souls touched with fire from the altar of God. Conversion of the human heart to God depends on neither Rock nor Bach nor Plainsong. Men and women holier than most of us have found God in cold, austere Cistercian churches, in Quaker meeting houses, and even in the still small voice that Elijah discovered after the wind, the earthquake, and the fire. Liturgy is not primarily a means of cajoling people to seek out God; it is, rather, the means of expressing the love that is already in the hearts of those whom God has touched in his own mysterious ways. That is why it is properly gorgeous.

Liturgy should be, indeed, a form of Christian wit, though of course it is also much else besides. By that I mean that it has a long history behind it of rigorous self-discipline bathed in human compassion. Neither religious literalists nor irreligious scoffers can possibly understand the true nature of its riches. It is the speech and gesture of the company of those whose faith has risen like a descant upon their doubts. The song of centuries of the triumph of those who, like the redeemed in the Apocalypse, have come out of great tribulation is not to be lightly exchanged to fit the mood of those who, like some of the Corinthians (I Corinthians 3:2), are still on a milk diet.

We have seen in earlier chapters how variegated is the function of Christian liturgy, how it is both work and art, old yet ever new for those who are willing to learn how to dig for its gold. Now we must see once and for all that it can be nothing unless it is flowing from a heart filled with love. And not for nothing do we talk of love and laughter as belonging to each other, inextricably bound together. The kind of laughter depends upon the kind of love, and many kinds there are. The love Christians celebrate has cost an unspeakable price. It does not issue in cheap

chuckles or loud guffaws, but in a merriment that is as
light and swift, as witty and winsome, as is the very movement of the Spirit of God.

These days when we have a theology of almost everything we can think of, there ought surely to be a theology
of mirth, to put before us in some systematic way the nature of Christian laughter. It might treat, for instance,
questions such as why Christians laugh at certain moments and in certain situations that others find too tragic
or too terrible for mirth. It is certainly not that Christians
fail to see the tragedy or underestimate its reality. It is,
rather, that they are peculiarly sensitive to the incongruity. Take, for instance, death. Death is the most terrible
ordeal that confronts every man and woman. Why, then,
are many of our funniest stories about funerals? The reason is plain. Death, as the existentialists have so clearly
seen, is absurd. Its absurdity calls attention to the ludi-
crous incongruity of human life. That furless and feather-
less biped we call man *is* absurd, and the absurdity is
accentuated by his attempts to forget it. He struts about
in this cosmic backwater we call Earth, able to be more
excited about reaching its nearby and apparently barren
satellite at fabulous cost in money than he generally is
about his own destiny and purpose. There is something
petty and trifling about him, too: he is often blind to the
grandeurs within him, yet infinitely concerned over what
is of least value in his own being. A rather diminished sort
of mammal with only two feet and trying to get one of
them off the ground and into heaven while trailing the
other over the open jaws of hell, he is above all *funny*. He
is never funnier than when death, which he has spent his
life trying to ignore, overtakes him and puts an end to all
his antics. To Christians death is the ever-present chal-

lenge to the folly of all our human pretensions, the supremely dramatic reminder of their absurdity and therefore of our absurdity whenever we turn our sights from God. Nothing, then, can be sillier or funnier than our futile attempts to cover up the consequences of our absurdity either by an ostrich-like pretense of the unreality of death or by ludicrously expensive funeral pomp.

Henri Bergson, in *Le Rire,* expounded a theory of laughter according to which the funniness of a situation consists in the abrupt stoppage of the stream of life by something lifeless or mechanical. A typical example would be that of a dignified man resplendent in a fine hat and elegant suit of clothes who suddenly slips on a banana skin. In death that situation is dramatized: the fine clothes are your human vanity and pride, the banana skin your body. Yet at the same time, for the Christian, death is also the moment of wonderment in which the Eternal most sharply intrudes upon the path of our life's pilgrimage. The authentic Christian finds in the situation a reason for both tears and laughter. He is deeply aware of the tragic quality of the situation; but he is aware no less of the angels' song rising in descant above the groans of the mourners around the already decomposing corpse. The combination of corporeal decay and spiritual grandeur seems indecent. If you think the grandeur illusory and the decay alone real, you may weep inconsolably. If you really believe, however, in the grandeur, you will see also a glorious absurdity. It will be somewhat as if you were witnessing an Olympic race in which the winner slipped at the last lap and involuntarily somersaulted across the finishing line. You will not be merely laughing at an incongruity: you will be celebrating a victory in a shout of love.

Love and laughter are so intertwined that you cannot
lose one without losing the other. They are like two halves
of a scissors. The laughter may be and generally is interior. It does not externalize itself as does buffoonery. Yet
it provides an excellent test of the health of a liturgical
act: Can you smile with God in prayer as you might smile
with a friend by the fireside or on a country walk?

The kind of laughter I have in mind is the kind that
springs from an immense inner confidence in the goodness
and providence of God and at the same time a profound
awareness of the absurdity of the liturgical situation.
Here am I, a poor bedraggled pilgrim along the path of
life, finding myself engaged in converse with the Foun-
tain of all things, the "Maker of Heaven and Earth." Here
am I, perhaps a physical weakling or a mental bore or a
moral cripple, talking of being joined by angels and archangels in the Church's song. Or else here am I, a great
mathematician or clever diplomat or famous architect, on
my knees in a tawdry chapel whose arrangement and fur-
nishings are in the worst possible taste, listening to music
that is off-key, and having to face a sermon that will re-
veal whole oceans of historical and theological ignorance
all in the course of a quarter of an hour. Why am I here?
How could I have found myself in this silly situation?
Only because I have come to believe with Jacob that "this
is none other but the house of God, and this is the gate of
heaven" (Genesis 28:17).

The incongruity that we noticed in considering the particularity principle confronts me at every point in the liturgical act, whoever I am and whatever I do. The oddity
of my own situation springs into focus, the grandeur and
the wretchedness that Pascal noticed in Everyman, the
gulf that the greatest classical theologians from Augustine

to Calvin have seen lying between the creature and his Creator. Unless I can see the absurdity and smile at it in love, I have not yet caught on to the miracle of the Mass, the adventure that is the Christian liturgy.

To laugh about religion (otherwise than as a mere hate-filled militant mocker) is to be at least on the fringe of religious belief. A person brought up in a totally "secular" environment, such as that of a modern totalitarian state, would not even see anything particularly funny about a good "Peter-at-the-pearly-gates" story. A "fringe" Christian, so long as he had got beyond the stage of being shocked at the notion of fun-filled faith, might chuckle nervously. Only a deeply devout Christian could laugh in love. Being inwardly convinced of the reality of the fuller life beyond the grave, he alone could find the notion of creaking heavenly doors and undergoing the scrutiny of Peter in the role of a celestial receptionist all the more ridiculous because it is a caricature of a profound reality in the destiny of man. Those wobblier in their faith might laugh; but their laughter would lack the moral serenity and the intellectual vivacity of the spiritually mature men and women whose merriment could pose no threat to their Christian assurance.

As every parish priest sooner or later discovers, his own spiritual survival depends more on the special sense of humor I am talking about than on any other single psychological endowment. If he saw nothing funny in the lamentations of Mrs. Jones, the arrogance of Mr. Smith, the neurotic venom of Miss Black, and the hebdomadal complaints of Mrs. White, he would perish. Such a priest needs a deep spiritual life if only that he may have, through it, the quality of humor necessary for his survival. The humor he needs is not the sort that could ever

minister to his personal vanity; still less is it cruel. It is the
kind that issues from his being able to see everything, but
especially the life of his parish, in a grander dimension, a
more telling perspective, *sub specie aeternitatis*. The need
of a sense of humor is not, of course, confined to the priest
in charge of a parish. It is the quality that is, more than
any other, desperately needed by every single member of
the congregation who is trying to develop an interior life
and be a real, if hidden, spiritual force in the life of the
parish.

The liturgy is the place above all others where Christian laughter must play its role. The half-Christians who
everywhere abound tend to see liturgy out of perspective.
That is true in every Christian communion that has anything like a liturgical structure. The enormous fuss they
make about extremely trivial matters could have only a
special combination of ignorance, narrowness, and neuro-
sis as its cause. The details of the liturgy, which should be
the expression of the deepest Christian love, come to be
the occasion of cantankerous wrangling and childish dis-
pute. In contemporary conditions, when the Church is, almost everywhere in the world, in the midst of a hostile society, the spectacle of Christians fighting about hymn
tunes and the correct shade of violet can surely bring only
ribald ridicule upon the long-suffering saints of God and
sorrow to their hearts. True, liturgical squabbles are no
doubt a very small part of the ecclesiastical wickedness
that grieves these sorely tried hearts; but it is peculiarly
shameful, since it concerns the most intimate relation in
which the Church can stand to her Redeemer. When people pick quarrels about picayune points and liturgical
minutiae, they give the same sort of impression one
would get from a family that squabble about their heir-

looms till they end by destroying them. Or else they look like children quarreling about how to address a present to their parents, with the result that it is never in fact sent, or is sent with evidences of struggle still clinging to it. Mature Christians smile at liturgical fuss, not because liturgy is unimportant but because, on the contrary, it is so important that fuss is inapposite and ineffective. Only when people are not really in love do they get uptight about trivia. As true lovers, being at ease with each other, laugh quietly at what the books tell them, so true worshipers, while they want to express their love in the most beautiful way the wisdom of the Church can devise, are ready to laugh gently at liturgical finickiness. Those who say they want to love more must learn to laugh more, for where laughter wanes love flies out the window.

Though liturgy is work, as we have seen in an earlier chapter, it is also the Christian's greatest joy. True, joy may be found in solitude, and tears in the midst of people; nevertheless, we generally seek a solitary place to weep and find joy in the company of our friends. Liturgy, which is nothing if not a corporate celebration, should reflect the kind of humble laughter that is the child of joy. It should silently invite loving hearts to Christ. Perhaps nothing is more needed at the present time to draw the young to church than the quality of laughter that only good liturgy can bring. For while young people today exhibit some splendid qualities that young people of earlier generations often lacked, the undisguised sadness of some young faces is their least reassuring feature.

Many who are unaccustomed to Catholic ceremonial hanker after what they call "a simple service." In one sense they are right. For they are detecting at least one truth about liturgy: people must be able to find simplicity in it, the simplicity of love. So, though such people fail to appreciate the riches the Catholic tradition places at the disposal of loving hearts, they are right in insisting on simplicity. Nevertheless I see nothing simple about those forms of worship that have lost the joy of Catholic ceremonial. Liturgical barrenness is no more purity of heart than is a papal High Mass. A Quaker meeting is certainly no less likely to be dull than is a Greek Orthodox service. Nevertheless, the longing for ease of movement, to have opportunity for the quiet prayer and deep interior recollection that certain forms of worship in the Reformed tradition provide, is healthy for a Christian, no matter what his tradition. What is always wrong is the false sanctimony and even ill humor that pervade some churches, not least but by no means exclusively churches in that same Reformed tradition. Once, in a village in Holland, I entered a Dutch Reformed church which, ten minutes before the hour, was already packed with a sea of uncannily clean, tidy, and unsmiling men and women. Reluctantly, someone directed me to a pew in which there was just room for me between a gentleman who might have been a Dutch caricature of Kierkegaard and a granite-faced woman who could have modeled for Van Gogh. These even more reluctantly made way for me as though their Christian charity and forbearance were being sustained by Stoic courage. In a place that seemed to smell of spiritual creosote, I felt about as welcome as an Internal Revenue agent at a meeting of Cosa Nostra.

Even in the less arid ecclesiastical climate in which I was nurtured, however, I had already had some experience of the tradition against laughter in religion. When I was ordained as a young clergyman in the Church of Scotland, one of my first pastoral calls had been on two elderly and dignified maiden ladies, the daughters of James Hutchison Stirling, whose book *The Secret of Hegel*, published in 1865, may be said to have introduced Hegel to Britain, putting the theology of the English-speaking world for long under an umbrella of Hegelian thought. One of the ladies was highly intelligent and conversationally animated. The other, whom the Victorian contemporaries of her youth would have accounted more womanly, hardly spoke. At last she broke her silence as tea was being poured.

"Doctor MacGregor," she remarked primly and unsmiling. "You are the first clergyman to have laughed in this house."

Of course I spontaneously burst into laughter at the accusation, thinking of the cavalcade of curates that must have passed through her family's drawing room from the time her father had been disclosing the secret of Hegel, each face rigorously unsmiling. Then, freezing slightly under her expressionless gaze as she awaited any comment I might have to make on her announcement, I inquired as earnestly as I could: "And Miss Florence, do you think a clergyman *should* laugh?"

After a moment of reflective hesitation, she replied decisively:

"Yes, Doctor MacGregor, I *do*."

Her attitude was not entirely wrong. There is a Christian self-discipline, a Christian ascesis in laughter, as in much else. Lord Chesterfield, in one of his letters, called laughter "low and unbecoming" and referred to "the shocking distortion of the face that it occasions." Loud laughter, he wrote, "is the characteristic of folly and ill manners." After assuring his correspondent that he was not a man of melancholy disposition and was as ready to

be pleased as anyone, he could affirm that "since I have
had the full use of my reason, nobody has ever heard
me laugh." [2] No doubt Chesterfield was thinking of what
Goldsmith called "the loud laugh that spoke the vacant
mind." [3] Christianity has taken up and transmogrified
well-bred Stoic restraint: laughter should not take possession of man, displacing fine feeling and lively thought, as
it does in the vulgar; yet joy and merriment can never be
far away from Christian action. "Merryment" comes from
the same Old English root as "mirth." There is nothing
sub-Christian in wishing people a merry Christmas. One
could not wish them saved without also wishing them
merry. The authentic Christian laugh is gentle. It is the
laugh of one who knows how brief is our earthly pilgrimage and how topsy-turvy are most of our human values,
not least in the Church.

So if an ill-trained acolyte lights the candles from the
wrong side of the altar or the priest reads the Epistle for
the wrong Sunday, no Christian need fume, as though the
Church's marriage to her divine Spouse were in jeopardy.
A good Christian smiles patiently and perhaps even quietly laughs. After all, a father whose prodigal son returns
at last does not chide him if he should spill the gravy from
the fatted calf. If he should as much as notice, he is likely
to find the mishap an occasion for quiet mirth rather than
a cue for grumbling.

Liturgy, though the act of Christian love, has an indi-
rectly didactic element in it, and the greatest teachers
have always understood the value of mirth in the communication of ideas. Milton remarked that "the vein of
laughing hath ofttimes a strong and sinewy force in

[2] *Letters,* March 9, 1748.
[3] Oliver Goldsmith, *The Deserted Village,* line 122.

teaching and confuting." [4] The Franciscans, who not only began their work by effectively teaching simple country-folk but within the century of their founding became the intellectuals of Europe, pre-eminent for their scholarship in the rising medieval universities, were affectionately called *joculatores Domini*, the Lord's jokers.

Indeed, if the sayings of our Lord as reported in the Gospels reflect anything at all of his original turn of speech, they attest a lively and often satirical wit, a witty speaking of the truth in love. "I have set before you many good deeds, done by my Father's power; for which of these would you stone me?" (John 10:32, NEB) is surely mirthfully ironical. Images such as that of feeding pearls to pigs, of a camel trying to get through the eye of a nee-dle, of straining off a midge and gulping down a camel, and of one blind man leading another and falling into the ditch together, all suggest a playful wit speaking the truth in love. Surely Christian worship should reflect something of that witty humility. The liturgy itself, drenched as it is in such biblical imagery, provides the basis; but liturgy, in order to be appropriated, must come to life in the minds and hearts of the participants. Doubt-less that takes most of us more than half a lifetime to achieve; but those responsible for the conduct of worship can help by entering into the debonair spirit of the lit-urgy. Blessed are the debonair, for theirs is the rhythm of God!

---

[4] John Milton, *Animadversions upon the Remonstrant,* preface.

Chapter VII

PRINCIPLES OF
CHRISTIAN LITURGY

God giving Himself through such apparently
slight vehicles, in such short moments, and under such bewilderingly humble veils.
    —Baron von Hügel,
      The Mystical Element in Religion

ONE conclusion at least follows from this study: liturgy
is not worth doing unless it must be done. It may as well
be abolished if any alternative is conceivable. If it were
no more than a useful, beneficial, or salutary exercise for
the Christian community, it could not be radically different from holding a jumble sale or going on a parish picnic, which are certainly useful, often beneficial, and sometimes even salutary activities.

What one thinks of the nature of Christian liturgy
depends on what one thinks of the Christian Church, as
what one thinks of the nature of the Christian Church depends on what one thinks of the nature of Christ. If you
think, as do many, that Christ was a man whose life and
teaching were so fine that those who are captured by his
message may fittingly worship the divine in him, when
they feel so moved, then you will see the Church as no

more than an obviously convenient vehicle for fulfilling that particular and laudable inclination. The church will then be as much the fitting place for worship as the college is the proper place for education. That is to say, one need not go to either place, though generally speaking, in the kind of society to which we have become accustomed, many feel that the two institutions still do the best jobs in their respective fields.

Nobody with any intelligence would suggest, however, that a person could not be educated unless he had gone to college. Some have been educated, often more effectively, in the school of life, and some claim to have educated themselves. Since, then, college is not indispensable, only a slight change in societal conditions and a fairly widespread recognition of that change would suffice to bring about its eventual abolition. With the aid of a dictatorial or crypto-dictatorial government, any society could abolish it in such circumstances almost overnight, and within the next year every journalist and cartoonist would be depicting it as a recent quaint survival just deceased. If that could be so easily done to education, which has always enjoyed considerable snob appeal among those outside the profession actually engaged in it, the elimination of the Church would be as easy as falling off a gargoyle. The destruction of the Church would not be averted by sentiment, however strong. The sentiment supporting several of the old British regiments was so strong that one might have thought their individual survival as well assured as that of Crown and Parliament together; yet they have been abolished and relegated, with duly tearful lament, to the picturesque annals of British military history. Unless the Church as a liturgical community means more than a society of people who, being great admirers of Jesus, have a deeply ingrained inclination to worship him and have been for long gratifying that admirable inclination, it could be written off no less easily by any decently organized state, perhaps even with the aid and guidance of the World Council of Churches, which would survive under a less outmoded name, such as the International Society of Christophiles.

In conclusion I would advance seven general principles of Christian liturgy. The first principle is: *liturgy must be done*. For a Christian community there can be no choice. Only in an empirical, nontheological sense can liturgy be defined etymologically as the work of the people. It must be understood, rather, as the work of God among his people. Through the Church, God's unique instrument, the liturgy exhibits the rhythm of God. That rhythm may take many forms, some flowing and discursive like the Greek, some terse and neat like the Roman. Yet, however embodied, the rhythm is unique. It is, like the Church, as distinctive as he who chose her to be his mystical Bride. All other principles may be seen to be corollaries of this first one.

The second principle is: *liturgy is not action but transaction*. Something takes place. Men and women do not merely foregather to see how beautifully they express their religious sentiments as they seek to take heaven by storm under the guidance of a priest experienced in that art. Still less do they come together to hear a preacher proclaim the gospel, which even if they were illiterate they could hear proclaimed on radio. Those who know what liturgy is come neither to perform a hallowed ritual act nor to warm their hands with others with whom they sing great pilgrim songs, though these are legitimate and often commendable endeavors. They come to take part in an ontological transaction in which God encamps awhile and man celebrates the divine self-giving of that encampment. The locus of the liturgy is, therefore, a place of business: God's business.

The third principle is: *liturgy is the supreme expression of the Church's faith, hope, and love.* This means that the individual participant should be able through the liturgy both to derive sustenance from the life of the Church and to make his own personal contribution to that life. The individual who participates in the Great Transaction should be able to feel he has at his disposal the riches of the whole Church from the earliest times to the present day. He should be able to feel that, in spite of the inevitable local peculiarities and diminishments, nothing is being withheld from him; that is to say, though not all can be given, he must find no barriers set up against anything that might be of value to him in the liturgical treasury of the Church.

The significance of that consideration cannot be easily overstated. Though a particular liturgical expression or performance may be for one reason or another gravely impoverished, it is still healthy so long as it does not close doors to me. It becomes unhealthy only when it closes doors in such a way that I go away feeling there has been a force at work to deprive me of part of my Christian heritage. So long as I do not feel thus impeded I may rest content in the knowledge that I can and ought to supply the deficiencies, so far as I can, from my own knowledge, experience, and imagination. Certain types of worship are indubitably constructed with a polemic intent to denigrate this or that aspect of the plenitude of Christian faith.

These are liturgically intolerable. Quite different are the shortcomings from which every human expression of the Church's faith, hope, and love must suffer.

The fourth principle is: *liturgy must cohere.* No less than every other work of art, it must have a structure. A poem is no less a poem because it is a lyric, an epic, or a sonnet; but it is a disaster if it tries to be all of these. As we have seen, there is nothing fundamentally wrong with doing the liturgy in local colloquial speech, as long as so doing it does not become the occasion for displays of arrogance or pride such as emasculate the worshiper's capacity to appreciate the wider and deeper riches of the Church's heritage. Nor is there anything wrong with a highly stylized, formal, and archaic speech and ritual. What is very wrong is the sort of concoction that plagiarizes chunks of the latter and incorporates with the plagiarism other chunks of ill-prepared contemporary-sounding jargon and modern-looking antics. No doubt the only thing really wrong with even that is that it springs from a rather conspicuously vulgar form of arrogance that is unattainable without positive dedication to the preservation of one's own ignorance; but that makes it wrong enough to make pillorying it right.

The coherence principle is admittedly a conservative one. By accepting it we commit ourselves to be extremely wary of "monkeying" with any liturgy that has proved itself to be a masterpiece of its own kind. I can listen reverently to aspirations such as, "Say, Jesus, you're a real cool cat"; but I boggle at effusions such as, "O God, forasmuch as without You we are not able to get along, mercifully grant that Your Spirit may jog us into action." By the same token, when I preach, on occasion, in a Black Baptist church, I welcome the almost litaneutical form of the interjections: "Thank you, Jesus!" "Praise the Lord!" "Alleluia!" Were somebody to come up with a "Hurray, hurray, gloria tibi, Domine," I should feel ill at ease.

I now come to the fifth principle: *liturgy is expression of the Eternal-in-the-Now, the Infinite-in-the-This.* As we have seen at an early stage of our study, liturgy, though it be also the work of the people, the common prayer, the universal sigh of the Household of Faith, is always the voice of God in a particular situation. Therein lies, indeed, much of the charm of any particular celebration. The mysteries are eternal; but they are "especially for this congregation here present." We hear about the little sodalities and leagues and unions of *this* parish; of the problems facing *this* congregation; of the particular individuals who need prayers, the people of whom nobody beyond the parish has ever heard but whose names are written in the Book of Life and whom we meet fleetingly at the altar of God. A stranger to the parish, I wonder who is this John Smith to whom the priest has casually referred, and who that Mary Jones at the mention of whose name a strange hush broods momentarily over the assembled flock. They, too, are among the "many" for whom the Blood of God is shed.

Yet all such particularizations are liturgically meaningless except in the context of the awesome antinomy of the presence and absence of God, apart from which there could be no manifestation of the particularity principle, since there would be nothing to particularize. That is why, in a dull and lifeless church service, the announcements only increase the banality, while in a rich and lively liturgical celebration they accentuate the poignancy of the whole transaction. Not even an intelligent skeptic can be unimpressed by the aching beauty of the traditional

practice of sandwiching the parochial chit-chat between
the splendor of the Gospel and the grandeur of the Creed.

I see the solemn little procession move northward, the
sputtering lights casting trailing blobs of gold on the pol-
ished stone below. As it winds its way up to the Gospel
ambo, the whole multitude around me rise like a great
wave under God's Boat that is the Church. I rise to my
feet with them, my faltering faith buoyed up by the
Household of Faith. The expectancy is punctuated by the
Byzantine formalities: the cantillation, the censing of the
Book, the jubilant wail rising like a great wind sweeping
through an opening in the forest: "Glory be to thee, O
Lord." Clouds of smoke are wafted heavenward while the
deacon of the Mass sings out the Gospel story appointed
for the day. The soldiers of Christ stand silent sentinels of
the faith for which martyrs have willingly died as others
tomorrow will die too. And then, as the Gospel slowly
winds to its triumphant ending, the cry goes up: "Praise
be to thee, O Christ." Then the thud of mortal flesh, the
sitting-down of the People of God.

Suddenly a priest at the chancel steps is chattering
away about how to get a copy of the *Holy Cross Bugle*,
from which one may learn the bus arrangements for the
Parish Picnic at Palmdale. The recent bazaar yielded 295
dollars and 13 cents; but more is needed to fix that leak
in the roof. Mrs. Jones is in the hospital with an ingrow-
ing toenail, and your prayers are asked for Carl Cronk,
the anniversary of whose death occurs about this time. The
whole avalanche of banalities belongs as much to the
rhythm of God, the splendor of the liturgy, as does the
Gloria in excelsis. And as the celebrating priest sweeps
upward again toward Sinai no less swiftly than he had
descended therefrom, every word of the glorious declara-

tion of the Church's faith has acquired new meaning and every meaning has become more easily appropriated in the light of the God-touched particularities of parish life.

So much for particularity. Now for the sixth principle: *liturgy entails creative restraint*. Whatever form liturgy takes, it is subject to the ascetic principle of all creativity: self-renunciation, self-restraint. Such restraint is as inseparable from it as it is from every other art form. It lies, indeed, at the very heart of God, the Creator, who in the exercise of his power is never wanton.[1] Every liturgical form should exhibit that central principle. Liturgical effectiveness is not easily achieved. Like the King James Version of the English Bible, whose authors bound themselves to rules that prohibited not only capricious change but all change that was not strictly required for accuracy in terms of the current textual knowledge, the liturgy of the Church should never be changed either for pedantry or for fads. I often think of the millions of uncomplicated but devoted people who, over the better part of a lifetime, have slowly and painfully learned the meaning the Church has called on them to see in her symbols, only to be peremptorily told that the whole system is to be updated to bring it into line with what liturgists and other experts think an improvement, or with what goes over well with the kids. I should rather be mistaken for a sloven by the former and a square by the latter than be even remotely responsible for the look of disappointment I have sometimes seen in the dying eyes of the devout.

Besides asking ourselves, as is so much the current vogue, what the traditional liturgical formalities can con-

[1] I have discussed this very profound question in my *Philosophical Issues in Religious Thought* (Boston: Houghton Mifflin, 1973); see especially pp. 385 f., 450 f.

vey to contemporary men and women and especially
young people, we should do well to ask another question:
What would a young Christian lad or girl from the days of
persecution have thought of it if, as his nerve was failing
him when he looked at the jaws of a lion, he could have
seen in a vision (as perhaps some were vouchsafed) the
stately Gospel procession, with candles and censing and
cantillation? The writer of the Apocalypse saw such a vision of heaven, and many were solaced by the hope of it
in trials such as not many of us have to face today in
witnessing our faith. But if someone whose faith was faltering in the midst of the Diocletian persecution could
have seen happening on earth what we are able to do in
any well-ordered parish today, proclaiming the triumph
of Christian freedom over Babylonian oppression, would
not he have gladly given his right hand to be present with
us? I submit that could we but speak for a moment with a
few such Christian boys and girls from that period, hear
the thrill in their voices and see the joy in their eyes as
they saw us do the Eucharist, we should soon be on our
knees to them begging for forgiveness for having been so
ready to tamper with the Chuch's treasures to please
those who today are sometimes reluctant to give up chew-
ing gum to watch one hour with our Lord. How they
would have shouted for joy to see grown men and women
fall to their knees at the words *et homo factus est*, "and
was made man," and how their eyes might fill with tears
on learning that we are departing from that usage so as to
be more "with" something we call "it."

The seventh and last principle I would specify flows
from all the rest, but more especially from the sixth that
has just been enunciated: *liturgy is the rhythm of God.*
That rhythm conforms to no human pattern. It is "wild."

It springs from the heart of God that beats forever in boundless *agapē*. It is, therefore, anything else other than static. Yet it has its own laws, as has the Bible, wherein the ways of God to man are pre-eminently disclosed and which is the basic constitutional document behind all Christian liturgical form. Many have discovered, as did the young Augustine, that the Bible does not measure well against any calculus of literary style, Ciceronian or Shavian, a Hemingway's or a Proust's. Yet its power is overwhelming. It is odd, irregular, surprising. Wherever the liturgy reflects the rhythm of God, it may be expected to have that same strange quality, at once fascinating, exasperating, and compelling, that any diligent student will find in the Bible. Nothing can really squeeze it into our mold, and the sooner a worshiper learns that, the sooner he will begin to hear the flutter of angels' wings between the comma and the word and see the Spirit of God himself sweep through the crumbling rood screen of his House.

Much of our nervous concern about the need for liturgical change springs from the false supposition that we are confronted with a question of strategy: how to get people to worship. In the history of religion that has never been the question to ask. The question has always been: What *kind* of worship is it to be? That will always be the question, for, incredible though it may sound to unwary ears, humankind is by nature so addicted to worship that if one god is unavailable it will always find another. The first of the Ten Commandments does not merely deprecate the worship of "other gods"; it assumes that if people do not worship this god they will worship that one. Notorious is the devotion of positivists and atheists to their chosen idols. "Religionless" Russians who would scorn the Tomb of Peter patiently line up to worship at the Tomb of Lenin. "Religionless" Americans who ridicule the worship of Mao see nothing funny in their own dedication to the cult of Mammon.

The question, then, can never be whether or not people are to worship. The question is what they will worship and what form the worship will take. A few decades ago we thought that calling sun-bathers sun-worshipers was rather a strained little joke; but the worship of the Sun, with full ritual gesture, has actually been revived in California as a serious cult. Who can deny that in recent years sex has come to be worshiped with a public and pagan fervor unmatched even by the ancients whose devotion to it so much disgusted those who had found the Christian Way? The Christian proclamation that through the Resurrection our Lord had triumphed over sin and death could have meant nothing if it did not include a profoundly anguished protest against the worship of sex and wealth and political power, a call to choose another and better focus of worship: the "One True God." It was a call to follow Christ as "our *only* hope": *ave crux, spes unica.* All authentic Christian worship must express that insistence that what we are doing excludes and makes idolatrous every other cult.

That is what our liturgy must make clear. The test of every liturgical change that is proposed must always be whether implementing the proposal would make it clearer. It is not enough that we should improve the sound of a cadence. Any gifted schoolboy could do that. Nor is it enough that we should provide an improvement in the rendering of an ancient liturgical text into the language of today. Any able young scholar in the field could

do that. The question is: Will this proposed change decisively express "our bounden duty" better than does the
existing formula?

The affirmation that Christian worship differs essentially from all other kinds of worship does not mean that
Christianity claims to have an exclusive admission ticket
to heaven, or to have the only key to God's bounty. That
is plainly by no means true. The claim is that Christianity
provides the answer to the particular question God has
graciously put into the minds of those whom he chooses,
through the anguish of life, to walk his way. In well-
designed multiple-choice questions there may be, as
students quickly learn, out of four possible answers, two
or three that are not at all foolish and that all seem, indeed, to fit. Yet only one fits perfectly. That is the kind of
answer the Christian Way has always provided. Worship
that fails to express the glory of the answer is too atten-
uated to pass muster. St. Augustine suggests that even as
a baby at his mother's breast he was unwittingly seeking
and finding the riches of God, which reach right into the
core of all things (*ad fundum rerum*);[2] yet he had not the
one right answer till it was given him by God after he had
tried several other fashionable alternatives.[3] Christian
worship is never and can never be anything but dull and
dismal and vain when it fails to express itself as a response to God rather than as a quest for him. Much of the
attitude of contemporary people leads them into a disas-
trous failure in worship, from every conceivable standpoint, simply because they assume they are supposed to
be engaged in a quest for God. They must be taught to

[2] Augustine, *Confessions*, 1.6.7.
[3] E.g., Manichaeism and Neoplatonism.

seek, rather, to appropriate what God has made so supera-
bundantly available to them in the riches of our liturgical
inheritance.

Yet when all that has been said we must note carefully
that appropriating the riches of God is no easy assign-
ment. Men and women have never done it without in
some way first making their own the whole history of
human striving, the great panorama of man's search, conscious and unconscious, for the means of salvation. The
instinct to worship has taken its toll in human sacrifice.
Men and women of bygone ages, exchanging their silks
and satins for rough sackcloth, and the pleasures of the
flesh for a prison diet and a hard bed in a cold and lonely
cell, did not learn without pain how to appropriate the
gifts of God. "Heaven is not winne with a wish," wrote
Zachary Boyd in the quaint seventeenth-century language
of *The Last Battell of the Soul*. People must be taught not
to expect to drop into church for inspirational enjoyment
as one drops into one's club to relax after a hard day. Only
those who have sorely hungered for that meeting of God
with man that is the liturgy can understand its glory or
know how reluctant must be the hands that seek to
change it without injury to its life. Only such people can
recognize the character of the answer that the liturgy
gives to man's question, because they alone know that it
was God who first gave them the question to ask. They
understand the rhythm of God because they come to it
running in love.

Of course that does not mean that others are totally incapable of appreciating *anything* in Christian liturgy.
Even the least trained mind, served by the dullest eye,
gets something out of the Parthenon as does the most un-
musical ear out of Debussy. There is no reason why a

Buddhist or Muslim should be unable to see beauty in Chartres. The fact that few even among physicists fully understand Einstein's theory of relativity certainly does not mean that they can make nothing of it at all. By the same token, anybody who has ever lived in any kind of structured community, even a village, can understand something of London and Paris and New York; but such a person could not understand London as a Londoner born and bred, or New York as a New Yorker, or Paris as one who has played as a child in the Parc Monceau or lived in the Place des Vosges. One may love liturgy in all sorts of ways and for all sorts of reasons, and so long as one does not suppose one has exhausted them all no harm is done. Still, there is a radical difference between "getting something out of" the liturgy, as a clever child might get something out of Kant or Browning, and grasping it at its core. To grasp the liturgy at its core one must first have been grabbed by God. Such a God-grabbed person, being by consequence madly in love with God, will use all his or her capacity to enter into God's rhythm. For such a person will have discovered that in that rhythm is to be found the lodestone of reality. No study of Bible or liturgy will ever seem oppressive to one who has fallen in love with God, to one who has been caught up into the divine rhythm. Such a man, woman, or child will study diligently, for "diligent" comes from the Latin verb *diligere*, "to take delight in," and such fortunate people inevitably delight in the liturgy, as the Psalmist delighted in the Law (Psalm 77:174; 119:70). They seldom are much in the way of longing for anything in it to be changed, not because they are unimaginative or obstinate but, on the contrary, because their love of God has made them able to find new life and new meanings over and over again. The liturgy, for such a person, is not a plot of land to be improved but, rather, a mine to be excavated.

James Joyce, in *Stephen Hero*, says something that may help us to understand what is at issue here. Joyce is referring to the "epiphanies" to which he alludes elsewhere: the sudden illuminations that give familiar objects new meaning. His *alter ego* finds even the clock of the Dublin Ballast Office "capable of an epiphany." He was for years in the habit of passing it often and of alluding to it as well as glancing at it. "It is only an item in the catalogue of Dublin's street furniture. Then all at once I see it and know at once what it is: epiphany. . . . Imagine my glimpses as the gropings of a spiritual eye which seeks to adjust its vision to an exact focus. The moment the focus is reached the object is epiphanized." Everyone who regularly and wholeheartedly participates in the liturgy has had some such experience, and whatever is the experience he has had touches him at the deepest possible level, for he is bringing his whole life to it.

We should now be able to see why tampering with the rhythm of God is so fraught with danger. The danger lies in the false attitude that is brought to the situation. It is not merely an unwillingness to mine God's gold. That might be due to nothing worse than carelessness or sloth. The trouble lies deeper, in the false conviction that one is really in the rhythm of God when one is as near it as is polka to plainsong. Our Lord did not chide the Pharisees for their blindness: "If ye were blind, ye should have no sin; but now ye say, We see; therefore your sin remaineth" (John 9:41). Liturgical masterpieces like the Roman Missal and the Book of Common Prayer are inexhaustible mines. Even after centuries of reverent devotion and scholarly critique we have not probed their depths. Even the most skillful and best-intentioned meddling may injure their integrity. Can we afford to raise up anything that might become an obstacle and diminish the disclosures that have startled men and women out of their misery and into the way of eternal life?

Much has been done, not only in an attempt to make the liturgy of the Church "acceptable" to "the new generation," but by way of watering down this or that liturgy in the interest of ecumenical *rapprochement*. Such aims may sound intrinsically laudable, as indeed their neglect is certainly sinful. Nevertheless, the methods may not match the aims, and too often that is a powerful factor in bringing about what Pierre Maury used to call "the ecumenical sadness." Genuine ecumenicity is never achieved at the expense of God's rhythm. Authentic Catholicity consists, as Yves Congar and others have emphasized, "not in the inclusion of unreconciled elements in one organization, but in the common relation of all to a given centre and ground of unity." [4] What is here said of the Church is preeminently true of the Church's song to God. A haphazard assembling of liturgical morsels ends up as cold and lifeless as an anthology of "Beautiful Thoughts from Ancient Authors," and the more its votaries shout and dance around it the more deathly it looks and feels. One is reminded of the incomprehension of those tourists who romp around the world and return with slides galore but are never quite sure whether "that picture" of the Basilique de Sacré Coeur is of something they saw in Istanbul or in Copenhagen.

All such phony eclecticism inevitably lacks the rhythm of God which, like the beauty of nature itself, is full of sur-

[4] A. G. Hebert, *The Form of the Church* (London: Faber and Faber, 1944), p. 101.

prises and never conforms to the fastidious artificiality of
our Esperantist expectations. The very phrase that a liturgical scholar frowned upon may be one that would speak
to a hungry soul, bearing the life-giving Spirit of God. The
very cadence that a reforming zealot has extruded as too
antiquated for the contemporary ear may be one that
would call a young man or woman out of the wilderness
of identity-seeking and into the marvellous light of him
whom to know is to have found one's identity forever.

I well remember an experience that is all too familiar to
every experienced preacher. As a neophyte I used to mark
what I took to be my "best" sermons so that I might use
them again and (such was my vain folly) perhaps even
one day publish the choicest. One miserable Sunday evening I preached one that afterward seemed to me to have
been from every possible point of view my worst. Besides,
it was raining and the congregation was both sparse and
weary. I went away ashamed and determined that in no
circumstances would I ever preach such a bad sermon
again. Perhaps I never did. Fifteen years later, however,
after I had come to the United States, a man called on me
whose face and name I vaguely remembered from the
past. He told me that something I had said in a sermon
had changed his whole life. He had become interested in
the work of the ministry, had gone in the intervening
years to Canada where he had taken a modified theological training and had eventually become the pastor of a
church. What was the momentous phrase? He could not
formulate it exactly; but he could give me the exact date
and place the sermon had been preached. I looked up my
old calendar and found it was that terrible sermon, the
one that had prompted my resolve never so to preach

again. Truly the Spirit of God "bloweth where it listeth," and that is by no means always on our "best" sermons or our most "perfect" liturgies.

Our first duty, then, as liturgists, is like our first task as preachers: not to stand in God's light, obscuring him when he comes in his mysterious power to his own, carrying the Food that makes men whole and speaking the Word that brings men back to life. As God often chooses strange, uncouth, and unlikely men to be his priests and so do the work of angels, so he often speaks and acts through liturgies at which scholars occasionally sniff and that worldly men and women scorn as being out of tune with the melody of their moment, out of time with the tempo of their hour.

Liturgies like that of St. John Chrysostom or the Roman Missal or the Book of Common Prayer are not merely the concoctions of a council or a committee. They come bearing the "wildness" of God. God gives them to us at least partly to show us how patient he is with us and how we, his priests and people, must be patient too. He gives them to us with all their defects, knowing and reminding us that the freight these frail vessels carry is an Ointment that caulks every seam in the Ship of God. In short, let us be cautious and very humble when we dare to try to improve upon what has fed the dearest of God's saints. If only priests and people kept in mind how sure is the Ointment the Church carries in their frail hands they would not be so much concerned about a solecism here or an archaism there. If only we appropriate the riches of what is given us, in such a way as to transform our lives, crowds will come running, and none will mind much about liturgical deficiencies in the Book of Common Prayer. By ap-

propriating Christ through our liturgical inheritance we
can surely lift him up high enough for all to see, and he
has promised: "I, if I be lifted up from the earth, will
draw all men unto me" (John 12:32).

Is not it possible that some of our eagerness to bring the
liturgy "up to date" may be due less to a zeal for souls
than to an itch to show how "with it" we are? George
MacLeod, founder of the Iona Community, used to tell of
how, when he was in charge of a well-heeled Glasgow
parish he was to make famous throughout Scotland, he
would go during the depression years to the local public
square to try to catch the Voice of the People. George,
always a magnetic orator, decided one day to get up on a
soapbox himself and preach Christ in a corner of the
square opposite the stance of the local Communist
speaker. As a result he was challenged to a debate. He
had two weeks to prepare, and he spent them frenetically
cramming all the information he could get about Dialectical Materialism and the like, so that he might stand his
own against his adversaries. The day duly dawned. The
debate took place with vigor, and George was on the top
of his form, as usual with more charisma than learning but
as always with devastating charm. Nobody, however,
asked him anything about Dialectical Materialism. Never
was he quizzed on *Das Kapital*. He might as well have
saved himself his self-imposed cram-course in Commu-
nism. For he was asked instead the most searching questions about the gospel. He soon began to wish he had
spent more of his time studying the text and its implica-
tions. He had thought to talk to his challengers "where
they were at." He had failed to see that though their
mouths were at Marx, their heart was at the gospel of our

Lord Jesus Christ. The application of the moral of that story to us and the Church's fringe and our liturgical heritage surely needs no exposition. A little girl, asked for a definition of a saint, and remembering the stained-glass windows in her parish church, replied, more wisely than she knew: "It's a person who lets the light through."

Liturgists are naturally prone to stress whatever element they think they find under-represented in the practice of their generation. Joy, for instance, has been a good candidate for emphasis in our time. So we have proposals for more hosannas and alleluias. Of course that is always salutary. When, however, the penitential element in our liturgy comes up for attack, apparently on the jejune supposition that there is something sad and morbid about bemoaning our sins, we may well wonder whether our liturgical reformers know what they are about. William Bradford, governor of Plymouth Plantation, tells us in his journal that the Pilgrim Fathers "sette aparte" a "solemne day of humiliation," a day of penitence and prayer, before ever they found occasion "*also*" (I quote his own word) to set apart the day of Thanksgiving that has become so much better known as a national festival.

Our elected secular representatives, much to their credit, have also shown themselves sensitive to the need for penitence: in 1973, during the Second Session of the Ninety-third Congress it was

Resolved by the Senate and House of Representatives of the United States of America in Congress Assembled, that the Congress hereby proclaims that April 30, 1974 be a National Day of Humiliation, Fasting and Prayer; and calls upon the people of our nation to humble ourselves as we see fit, before our

Creator to acknowledge our final dependence upon Him and to repent of our national sins.[5]

Have we no reason to fear that the Church may be giving less spiritual leadership at this point than is the Congress of the United States? There are obviously some things we need not pray for in certain circumstances: Oregonians rarely need the Collect for Rain or Californians the one for Fair Weather; but when and by whom is an act of contrition properly omitted? Our sins are spread all over the press; they flash across every television screen in the nation. Perhaps, indeed, we might better appreciate the role of penitence in Christian liturgy if, during Holy Week, the Crucifix were covered, not with a violet veil but with a mosaic made up of the front pages of our national newspapers. Then might we better understand that peculiarly Christian acclamation that occurs in the long hymn, *Exultet jam angelica*, sung by the deacon at the blessing of the paschal candle on Easter Eve in the Latin Church, for which I would propose the slightly unconventional rendering: "O fruitful offense that deserved a Redeemer such as this!" [6]

That cry of joy and anguish expresses in a paradox the profound and peculiarly delicate Christian experience of God as at the heart of all things. Sin is real and abhorrent; but it is part of the human drama of love and strife. God

[5] *Congressional Record, Proceedings and Debates of the 93rd Congress, Second Session.*

[6] *O felix culpa, quae tantum et talem meruit habere Redemptorem.* This theologically profound notion finds expression in a well-known late medieval English carol, "Adam lay ybounden." (*The Oxford Book of Carols*, no. 180). It is known to music lovers today in Benjamin Britten's *Ceremony of Carols* in which it appears under the title "Deo Gracias."

is at work in that drama of the human plight, and because
his love is infinitely grander than ours, so is its cost infinitely greater to him than anything can be to us. God
does not merely share our burdens or heave them onto his
infinitely supportive shoulders. He struggles in, with, and
through the idiotic follies and hideous injustices of our
human predicament and suffers the excruciating torture
of them all throughout his victory over them.[7] So when in
the liturgy we offer the Christian sacrifice in, with, and
through Christ, we dare do so only because he is working
out his love in, with, and through us. Our liturgy must be
at every point an acknowledgment of that love.

It is also an acknowledgment of the presence of all who
have been involved in the torture and the triumph: the
Communion of the Saints! A strange and motley crew indeed, from Cain and Abel to Aunt Matilda and Uncle Jim!
Tears and laughter are equally apposite; but both are
transfigured by the laughter and the tears of God whom
we are encountering in the exercise of his agapistic
power. The Parish Eucharist can never be merely parochial nor the Family Eucharist merely familial, for the
family is God's whole family and the parish boundaries
extend not only to the ends of the earth and the uttermost
reaches of space but throughout all time. And so as we
utter the Commemoration, "And we also bless thy holy
Name for all thy servants departed this life in thy faith
and fear," we are united with men and women who have
gone beyond this particular arena of the drama of salvation
from sin and from the struggle with human stupidity and

[7] Theologians will please note (*a*) that my view does not imply a
Timaeus understanding of creation, and (*b*) that I attend elsewhere in
my writings to the possibility of a technical charge of patripassianism.

folly. Here, if anywhere, we can and do meet those, our
loved ones, who have meant most to us on earth. All this
can come over to us far more strikingly in a little make-
shift chapel than in a great cathedral. Father Schmemann
attests how "in the first years of the Russian emigration,
when worship had to be celebrated in cellars and garages
converted into churches, we became aware of the complete impossibility of celebrating it 'as it should be,' according to all the canons of elegance and solemnity
proper to the synodical style of Russian Orthodoxy," yet
these "wretched garage churches will remain forever connected with the fullness of liturgical experience, something
which becomes impossible in churches of magnificent and
grandiose design." [8] The rhythm of God is often less audi-
ble in St. Peter's Basilica than when Mass is said in a
lean-to in the fish market.

*   *   *   *   *

It is still half dark in the chilly hut that is serving as a
church, and rain is falling hard on the corrugated tin
roof. Two tall tapers are aflame on the altar, symbolically
proclaiming the light of Christ in the world, "a light to
lighten the Gentiles" and "the glory of thy people Israel."
Half a dozen old women with shawls over their heads, a
man in a business suit, a lanky teenage boy, and a couple
of smartly dressed women are kneeling in their places behind rickety chairs while a scrabble of little acolytes in
dumpy cottas and crumpled red soutanes are bumbling
their way back to the sacristy. A few more people with
dripping umbrellas are wiping their feet resolutely on the
remaining bristles of an old mat at the door. An old man

[8] Alexander Schmemann, *Introduction to Liturgical Theology* (London: The Faith Press, 1966), pp. 92 f.

with a sad face is now ensconced in a corner, his big
leathery hands clasped under his weather-beaten chin.
His lips are moving slightly in prayer. A pretty young
woman is staring earnestly, her eyes shiny pools under
arches of mascara. The damp air is heady with expectancy. The holy silence that broods gently over the
kneeling figures is broken only by the genuflections of an
increasing volume of people, till at length the chairs are
all taken and a few latecomers are crouching by the wall.

As the Holy Eucharist begins, there is a sudden sense of
action. Something is happening: not even a bewildered
visiting Martian could fail to notice that! God's army is on
the move, marching to the beat of his heart. You can feel
the presence of unseen hosts hovering among us as the
drama of the Mass unfolds. The awesome words are uttered and we become "partakers of his most blessed Body
and Blood," as the love of God moves out crisply among
the slush of drab humanity in the swift, white flakes of the
sacrament of his love. *Agnus Dei!* "Lord, I am not worthy
that thou shouldest come under my roof." Quickly the
great action is concluded. He has been and gone. . . . He
has been and stayed. The priest, having blessed the kneeling crowd, clasps to his breast the covered chalice and
swirls out through a plywood door. The faithful stay for a
moment for a last private greeting to God. The candles are
extinguished and, after a rustling here and a hobbling
there, the church is empty again, beautified by nothing
that man has done but radiant with the mystery of the
Real Presence in motion. For a fleeting moment one
thinks how different the liturgy should be, with seven
deacons and all the ceremonial splendor that loving hearts
always want to bring to God. Yet, after all our wistfulness
for the ancient beauty has passed, we ask ourselves

whether our liturgy in this shabby little shed has lacked anything, and even in asking the question we perceive that the answer is No.

For the rhythm of God is not our rhythm. True, it does not come ready-made from heaven. It is too subtle for that. It has indeed been edited and adapted and revised, as has the Bible itself, at the hands of men; but let us beware what hands of ours touch it, lest it bypass our encampment. It does change, but slowly, and not for the pleasure of a sophomore or at the learned whim of a liturgical committee. The Church is certainly called to review and sometimes even to revise liturgical solecisms and anachronisms, even those that have played a great part in her heritage; but she dare not shirk her responsibility of making sure, by long and earnest prayer, that she is not trying to clarify God's mind for him or tidy up his ever-surprising and inimitable rhythm.